Access to Information in the European Union

Europa Law Publishing, Groningen 2005

Access to Information in the European Union

A Comparative Analysis of EC and Member State Legislation

H. Kranenborg & W. Voermans

Europa Law Publishing is a publishing company specializing in European Union law and international public law.
For further information please contact Europa Law Publishing via email: info@europalawpublishing.com or visit our website at: www.europalawpublishing.com.

Typeset in Scala and Scala Sans, Graphic design by G2K Designers, Groningen/Amsterdam

NUR 828; ISBN 90-76871-46-9

British Library Cataloguing-in-Publication Data
A catalogue record for this book is available from the British Library

Preface

In September 2004, the Dutch Ministry of the Interior and Kingdom Relations commissioned us to make an inventory of the transparency legislation of the 25 Member States of the EU and to make a comparative analysis of the data. The results of the project were intended to encourage discussion during the EU Conference 'Transparency in Europe – II', organised by the Dutch EU Presidency, held in The Hague on 25 and 26 November 2004. Thanks to the wonderful and active cooperation of our *rapporteurs* we managed to construct a rather comprehensive overview of Member State legislation and to produce a concise comparative analysis in the relatively short period before the conference.[1] Following the Conference, we decided to further elaborate on the research. In addition to improving the inventory of Member State legislation, we added general EC-legislation on access to documents. We extended the comparative analysis by including EC legislation.

With this book we try to kill two birds with one stone. Our first aim is a practical one, namely to provide for a rough but comprehensive overview of EC and Member State legislation concerning access to information. In order to improve the practical value of this publication, a website was created that contains a digital version of Part III, the EU and Member State Survey. All the hyperlinks in the footnotes are available via the website. These hyperlinks make it possible to directly consult the English translations of national legislation (if available). The website can be found at: http://www.transparencyineurope.leidenuniv.nl. The second aim of our book is of a more academic nature. We have tried to assess what conclusions can be drawn from the comparison of EC and Member State legislation. Two questions are addressed in particular: are there any general differences between the 'old' and the 'new' Member States? And, secondly, is the EU more or less transparent then the 'average' Member State?

At this stage, research on Member State legislation must be seen as an initial inventory. Although we have tried to be as comprehensive as possible, we can merely highlight the characteristics of the different legal regimes of the Member States. In most cases, we could not delve into national practice and based ourselves solely on legislation. Therefore, we probably did not always succeed in pinpointing the most prominent provisions. For that reason we strongly invite the reader to send comments and suggestions in order to improve our research. This can be done via e-mail or via the aforementioned website. The Member State Survey was concluded on 1 March 2005. The whole book was finalized on 15 May 2005.

The research underlying this book contributes to the E.M. Meijers Institute's research program *'Securing the rule of law in a world of multilevel jurisdiction'*

---

[1] The contributions to the Conference are published in H.R. Kranenborg, P.J. Stolk, A. Tunovíc & W.J.M. Voermans (eds.), *Transparency in Europe II*, 2005, ISBN 90541 40925.

at the University of Leiden Faculty of Law. We would like to thank the Dutch Ministry of the Interior and Kingdom Relations for their initiative that resulted in this book. We are further grateful for the copy-editing assistance of Angelynn Meya and the assistance of our student-assistant Mieke van Ulden. We finally would like to thank the Europa Instituut of the Leiden Faculty of Law for their support.

Herke Kranenborg (h.r.kranenborg@law.leidenuniv.nl)
Wim Voermans (w.j.m.voermans@law.leidenuniv.nl)

Leiden, May 2005

Contents

PART I

Introduction

'In all my public and private acts as your president, I expect to follow my instincts of openness and candor with full confidence that honesty is always the best policy in the end.'

Gerald R. Ford

§ 1 Introduction

This book is about transparency in Europe, by means of access to government information. Transparency is becoming increasingly important in modern democracies, especially in a new democracy like the European Union. Stable democracies are based above all else on trust, public trust. While in the past, confidence in governments was based on control by elected representatives and was a matter-of-course, this no longer holds true for post modern democracies. The idea of representative democracy has proven fallible, and public trust in democratically controlled governments is no longer self-evident. Transparency is one way of filling the widening gap of so-called 'democratic deficits' which by no means is a phenomenon unique to the European Union. Transparency is often portrayed as the heal-all, wonder potion to problems facing modern governments. This book will not try to answer the question whether transparency is an effective remedy for the ailments of modern democracies, but will focus in a comparative way on the legal regimes of EU countries and the EU regarding access to information. In this book, which is the amalgamated result of our own research and the findings of a 2004 European Conference on Transparency, we will make a tour of access to information legislation in European countries and see whether something can be learnt, by way of example, contrast, comparison or simple illustration, from these European systems. A first step, is a basic analysis of those legal regimes.

§ 2 Defining the Scope of the Research

Our research focused only on one aspect of transparency, namely access to documents. In particular, in the national regimes we narrowed the scope to documents held by *government* bodies; we did not address the topic of legislation pertaining to access to documents held by the judiciary or legislature. However, as can be seen in the EU and Member State Survey, Part III, this distinction is not always clear.

The research was further restricted to *general* legislation on access to documents. In a majority of Member States, access to environmental information and personal data is governed by separate legislation. This legislation stems mainly from European legislation. Access to environmental information is addressed by

Directive 90/313/EEC[1], which was repealed by Directive 2003/4/EC on 15 February 2005.[2] The latter directive implements the obligations formulated in the Århus Convention, which was signed by the EC in 1998.[3] Access to personal data forms part of the rules on protection of personal data as laid down in Directive 95/46/EC.[4] The present study did not attempt to examine separate regulations pertaining to environmental and personal information. Only where these issues were addressed in provisions of the general legislation on access to documents have they been included.

The study does not examine how access to information relates to national rules on freedom of expression. This subject falls outside of the scope of the present research. Only with regard to Malta, which is one of the three countries without legislation in the field of access to information, has the relationship between freedom of expression and the right to access documents been briefly discussed, including an analysis of the European Court of Human Rights case law regarding Article 10 of the European Convention on Human Rights.

§ 3 Methodology

In discussing the EU regime on access to documents, relevant legislation as well as case law of the Court of Justice has been analysed. Information on the practical implementation of EC legislation was based on a report of the European Commission presented in January 2004 which evaluates implementation of the principles of access to documents.[5]

For the Member State survey, we have only analysed relevant *legislation*. Case law on the practical application of the law is generally not accessible in English. Additionally, in many cases statistical facts are not obtainable. For these reasons, the survey and analysis with regard to the Member States are theoretical in nature. Naturally, the true effectiveness of access to information laws can only be determined through their practical application.

Data was compiled firstly through answers to a questionnaire that was sent to different country representatives which took part in the EU Conference 'Transparency in Europe II'.[6] The Internet was a second source of informa-

---

1 OJ 1990, L 158/56.

2 OJ 2003, L 41/26.

3 The Århus Convention can be found at http://www.unece.org/env/pp/documents/cep43e.pdf.

4 OJ 1995, L 281/31.

5 See Commission-report on the implementation of the principles in EC Regulation 1049/2001, COM(2004) 45 final, this report can be found at http://europa.eu.int/eur-lex/en/com/rpt/2004/com2004_0045en01.pdf. Below, this document is referred to as 'Report of the European Commission of 30 January 2004'.

6 The answers of the representatives of Austria, Belgium, Estonia, Finland, Germany, Hungary, Italy, Latvia, Malta, Poland, the Slovak Republic and Slovenia are processed.

tion. Most countries have made English translations of legislation on access to documents available on the Internet; as far as we know, Lithuania and Spain are the only exceptions. The EU and Member State Survey, Part III, references all relevant addresses on the World Wide Web; these were accurate through 15 May 2005. We have also used existing surveys on national legislation on access to information. The 'Overview of Member States' National Legislation Concerning Access to Documents', created by the European Commission in 2000, proved very useful.[7] Another valuable document was 'The freedominfo.org Global Survey', which was written by David Banisar and completed in May 2004.[8] The last source of data worth mentioning are the results of a questionnaire that was posted last year under the auspices of the Council of Europe. This questionnaire was drawn up by the Steering Committee for Human Rights in order to foster the discussion within the Council of Europe on the question of whether Recommendation Rec(2002)2 on access to official documents should be transformed into a legally binding instrument.[9] Upon request, the Secretary of the Steering Committee sent these results to us.[10] Of course, in footnotes we have referred to the specific literature that we used.

§ 4 Terminology

As noted above, research was restricted to 'government bodies'. We also used the notion of 'public authority' or 'administrative authority'. Within the scope of the research, these words are interchangeable. Although the consequent use of a single notion would make the EU and Member State survey easier to read, we felt obliged to use the wording chosen in the English

---

7 See document SG.B.2/VJ/CD D(2000) of 9 October 2000, to be found at http://europa.eu.int/comm/secretariat_general/sgc/acc_doc/docs/apercu_en.pdf. Below, this document is referred to as 'Report of the European Commission of 9 October 2000'. Another document we used of the European Commission was document SG/616/03-EN of 1 July 2003, containing a comparative analysis of the Member States' and candidate countries' legislation concerning access to documents, to be found at http://europa.eu.int/comm/secretariat_general/sgc/acc_doc/docs/compa_en.pdf. Although useful, it appeared to be less extensive than the former Commission document.

8 See D. Banisar, Freedom of Information and Access to Government Record Laws around the World, May 2004, published on http://www.freedominfo.org. Below, this document is referred to as 'The freedominfo.org Global Survey of May 2004'.

9 Recommendation Rec(2002)2 can be found at http://cm.coe.int/stat/E/Public/2002/adopted_texts/recommendations/2002r2.htm.

10 The results of the questionnaire, known as document DH-S-AC(2004)001 add, and other information on this topic can now be found at the website of the Steering Committee for Human Rights, see http://www.coe.int/T/E/Human_rights/cddh/. Below, the results of the Council of Europe questionnaire are referred to as 'the results of the Council of Europe questionnaire'.

translations of the national laws. In principle, also the words 'information' and 'document' are interchangeable, although we are aware that the word 'information' has a broader meaning than the word 'document'. We will discuss these differences in wording used in different national legislation only with regard to the question of whether an applicant may either request *information* or must specifically indicate the requested *documents*; in other words, whether a country makes use of an information or document-based system.[11]

The legal basis of the rules on access to documents is Article 255 EC Treaty. The regulation on access to documents is therefore *EC* legislation. However, these rules also apply to documents held by the institutions which relate to activities of the European Union. Therefore, in general terms we speak about the *EU* regime on access to documents. If we refer to specific legislation, a reference is made to the EC.

§ 5 Structure of the Book

In addition to this introduction, the research consists of a comparative analysis of EC and Member State legislation (Part II) and the EU and Member State survey (Part III). All descriptions of European and national legislation follow the same pattern. They all start with an indication of the relevant legislation on access to information. Then the scope of the legislation is given, after which the point of departure is formulated. After a description of the exceptions, the procedural rules are presented. After that, the legal remedies are indicated and – if present – the institutional structure is given. Most of the surveys are concluded with some remarks on 'other characteristics'. This allowed us to highlight some particular features of the legislation. The comparative analysis of EC and Member State legislation follows a similar structure.

11 *Infra* Part II, § 7.

PART II

Comparative Analysis

§ 1 Introduction

In this analysis, we have tried to highlight the common features, the most striking differences and the noteworthy characteristics of the various Member State regimes on access to information. To that, we have added the most interesting insights that emerged from discussions during the EU Conference 'Transparency in Europe – II'. We also added the main features of relevant EC legislation, in order to make a comparison between national and EC legislation.

The analysis starts with a few remarks on the formal relationship between EC and national legislation (§ 2). It then presents thoughts on the multi-layered character of the principle of access to information (§ 3). In § 4, general remarks are made on existing legislation in the field of access to information. The analysis proceeds by examining the scope of the legislation (§ 5) and exceptions (§ 6). In § 7, the procedural requirements that applicants and public authorities must fulfil are described in general; § 8 is dedicated to legal remedies. This is followed by remarks on the institutional structure (§ 9) and certain other characteristics of the national laws (§ 10). Finally, the conclusion addresses whether general differences exist between the 'old' and the 'new' Member States and whether the EU is more or less transparent than the 'average' Member State (§ 11).

§ 2 The Formal Relationship between EC and National Legislation

The EU or the EC has no competence to harmonise national rules on access to documents. The European regulation on access to documents only concerns access to documents held by European institutions. However, the regulation has some influence on national legislation, where it deals with documents held by national authorities originating from a European institution. Where a Member State is requested to disclose such a document, the Member State must – in case of doubt – consult the institution before disclosure. This obligation may lead to amendments in national legislation. The present research does not address the legal validity of this issue.

On the other hand, where a document originates in a Member State and is held by one of the institutions, the Member State can request the institution not to disclose the document without its prior consent. Absent such a request, the general rule on access to documents originating from third-parties applies: the institution must – in case of doubt – consult the third party in order to assess whether one of the exceptions in the EC regulation applies.[1]

[1] *Infra* Part III, European Union, p. 33-34.

§ 3 Access to Information: A Multi-layered Principle

Access to information is an important principle in all Member States. It performs different functions in rule-of-law based democratic governments. It also serves different goals. The principle of access to information is truly multi-layered. Firstly, in many countries it appears as a legal principle. Access of information legally establishes the public's right to know, and – sometimes in a mirror image way – obliges the government to inform the public. The legal right or duty to obtain or provide information aims to create transparency (hence the principle of transparency) which in turn assures certainty in government and safeguards against arbitrariness. Secondly, the principle of access to information – in most countries – is a democracy amplifying principle. Whether or not legally enshrined in this respect, it seeks to promote citizens' participation in government decision- and policy-making. At the same time, transparency offers the opportunity to influence and control government action and thus, prevents corruption or other aberrations. In this way, transparency may contribute to the legitimacy of government policies and decisions. In the third and final layer, access to information accords with the principle of good governance. Transparency can and does improve communication between the government and the public, and the government and stakeholders in government policies. Good, well targeted information can act as a lubricant to decision-making processes. Seen from this angle, transparency may boost efficiency, promote legitimacy and assist in smooth implementation.

The fact that the principle of access to information is multi-layered does not automatically imply that all three layers are equally present in the regimes of all Member States. It does, however, show that elements of the different layers can and do co-exist simultaneously in many Member States and that the layers of the principle build on one another.

§ 4 Legislation on Access to Information

A Fundamental Right of Access to Documents?

At the European level, discussion exists as to whether the right of access to documents, as laid down in Article 255 EC Treaty and Regulation 1049/2001, is of a fundamental nature.[2] Can one speak of a fundamental right or human right to access to documents in the European legal order? According to Article 6 EU Treaty, the Union shall respect fundamental rights 'as they result from the constitutional traditions common to the Member States'. For this

[2] See amongst others D.M. Curtin, *Citizens' fundamental right of access to EU information: an evolving digital passepartout?*, in *CMLRev.* 2000, p. 7-41 and R.W. Davis, *Public Access to Community Documents: a Fundamental Human Right?*, in *EIoP* 1999, vol. 3, to be found at http://eiop.or.at/eiop/pdf/1999-008.pdf.

reason, it is interesting to note that ten of the 24 countries with a constitution have enshrined the right of access to documents in their constitutions.[3] In the constitutions of Austria, the Czech Republic, the Slovak Republic and Spain, accessibility of documents is formulated as a *duty* for public authorities rather than as a right for individuals. However, the duty of authorities to provide access to documents can constitute a right for individuals to access documents when individuals can hold an authority accountable for failure to perform. Of the remaining countries, their constitutions are silent on access to documents.

Within the European Union, things will change once the Treaty establishing a constitution for Europe becomes law. The Treaty addresses the right of access to documents twice. First, the right can be found in Article 50 of the first part of the Treaty. This article is the equivalent of Article 255 EC Treaty, which is the legal basis of Regulation 1049/2001. This legal basis will move from a title near the end of the EC Treaty called 'provisions common to several institutions' towards a position in the first part, considered as the constitutional part of the Constitutional Treaty, under the heading 'the democratic life of the Union'. Secondly, the right of access to documents is one of the rights contained in the Charter of Fundamental rights, which as part II will be included integrally in the Treaty.

Secondary Legislation on Access to Information[4]

A substantial majority of Member States has specific acts on general access to information. In a few countries, general rules on access to documents are part of legislation of a broader scope. For instance, in Greece and Spain access to documents forms part of the general law on administrative procedure. In Sweden, rules on access are laid down in the Freedom of the Press Act, which forms an integral part of the Swedish Constitution. In the EU, Regulation 1049/2001 is a specific act on general access to documents.

In Germany, an act on freedom of information at the federal level is expected to enter into force in mid-2005. Until then, federal legislation is absent and only four of the *Länder* have legislation in the field of access to public documents. Cyprus, Luxembourg and Malta do not have any legislation on general access to information.

Ten out of 24 national constitutions grant *a* right to individuals to access information, and this amount is increased by six if we include secondary legislation.[5] Moreover, secondary legislation in Latvia and the United Kingdom states

---

3 Belgium, Estonia, Finland, Greece, Hungary, the Netherlands, Poland, Portugal, Slovenia and Sweden. In the case of Slovenia, only individuals with a well-founded legal interest can invoke this right. The United Kingdom is evidently missing from the list of ten, since it does not have a written constitution.

4 Secondary legislation is understood here as subordinate legislation, i.e. not laid down in a constitution or a parliamentary act.

5 France, Ireland, Italy, Lithuania, the Slovak Republic and Spain. In the case of Italy, only individuals with a personal concrete interest have the right to access administrative documents.

that individuals are 'entitled to obtain information' (Latvia) or are entitled to have information communicated to them (United Kingdom). Also in the *secondary* law of the Czech Republic, a right for individuals does not exist. However, a duty to provide information does in many cases correspond with a right for individuals, where the law states that public authorities have to provide information in response to an individual's application. The Austrian Federal Information Act states that anyone may *ask* for access to information, and the Danish Act states that 'any person may demand that he be apprised of documents'.

§ 5 Scope of Legislation

Beneficiaries

Most Member States that grant individuals the right of access to documents either through their constitutions or secondary legislation grant this right to everyone, including foreigners and legal persons. In some countries, this right is only given to persons having a specific interest. In Italy, one has to have a 'personal concrete interest to safeguard in legally relevant situations' and in Slovenia applicants have to show 'a well founded legal interest'. In Greece, the right seems to be granted only to *interested* parties. It is unclear whether an applicant must actually show a specific interest. Case law of the Greek Council of State seems to suggest that a justified interest is required. On the other hand, the Greek Committee that prepared the relevant law stated that no legal interest need be proven. In Latvia, a distinction is made between generally accessible information and restricted information. The former will be disclosed to anyone wishing to receive it, while only individuals who describe the specific purpose for which the information will be used can gain access to restricted information. Lastly, Spain seems to grant the right to access to documents only to Spanish citizens.

Article 255 EC Treaty and Regulation 1049/2001 limit the group of beneficiaries to any citizen of the Union, and any natural or legal person residing or having its registered office in a Member State. However, the regulation creates the possibility for the institutions to extend the group of beneficiaries to natural or legal persons not residing or having its registered office in a Member State. All three institutions used this possibility.

Official Documents

The meaning of the term 'document' is defined in many different ways. In the broadest sense, it refers to any information available in whatever format. Some countries limit the definition to finalised documents, excluding preparatory documents from the scope of access.[6] Sometimes special rules apply to documents drawn up for internal use ('internal documents'). In the Netherlands, for example, no information is disclosed concerning personal opinions on policy contained in internal documents.[7] A few Member States provide a list of documents that are not considered (official) documents. Portugal, for example, excludes personal notes, memos and other records of a similar nature.[8] On the other hand, Hungarian public authorities are obliged to 'create' documents, by making notes on any information received by word of mouth that is important to a pending decision and which is not already contained in a document. The Danish law explicitly states that the right to access also applies to duplicate copies of letters issued by an authority.

Rules on access to documents mostly apply to *official* documents. In general, this means documents *held* by public authorities, including documents *originating from* and *received by* a public authority. Greek rules on access to documents are an exception. In principle, these rules only apply to documents *drawn up* by a public authority. These so-called 'public documents' are different from 'private documents'. The latter are only accessible by individuals who have a specific case pending before the public authority holding the documents and to whom the documents relate. Some countries explicitly restrict access to documents that *relate to the course of activities* of a public authority.[9] In the Czech Republic and the Slovak Republic, the obligation to disclose information upon request applies only to documents that regard an authority's decision-making power.

A few Member States provide a non-exhaustive list of what is meant by 'official documents'. The disclosure of these documents is mandatory.[10]

Regulation 1049/2001 gives a general definition of what is considered as a document: any content whatever its medium (written on paper or stored in electronic form or as a sound, visual or audiovisual recording) concerning a matter relating to the policies, activities and decisions falling within the institution's sphere of responsibility. Inter-

---

6 See for example France and Spain. In Finland, preparatory documents only fall within the scope of the law when these documents contain such information that they are to be archived in accordance with national legislation.

7 Other countries having special rules on internal documents are *inter alia* Denmark, Estonia, Latvia and Sweden.

8 See also Finland.

9 See for instance Denmark.

10 See for instance Poland, the Slovak Republic and Slovenia.

nal documents fall within this definition, albeit a special exception applies. The right to access applies to documents held by the institutions.

Public Authorities

'Public authority' is also defined in a variety of ways. Member State legislation tends to define these authorities in two ways. Firstly, a general definition may be given as to what constitutes a 'public authority'. Secondly, national legislation may provide for a list of bodies that it considers 'public authorities'.

Most countries provide a general definition. To speak in terms of the well known theory of the separation of powers, 'public authority' is generally perceived and defined as the 'executive'. The judiciary and legislature are exempted. Some exceptions do, however, exist. In Finland, courts are included in legislation on access to documents; in Lithuania and Poland, political parties are also considered to be 'public authorities'. The notion of 'bodies belonging to the executive', however, requires further clarification. In this respect, Member State laws vary in scope from narrow to broad. The scope is narrow if, for instance, 'public authorities' is restricted to bodies that are created in accordance with public law.[11] A broad interpretation is given when 'public authorities' includes private bodies performing an administrative function[12] or financed with public funds.[13] Some countries even go further including trade unions[14], banks[15] and non-profit organisations that are in some way supported by the government.[16]

Ireland, Slovenia and the United Kingdom have chosen to list all relevant authorities with the possibility of expanding the list. In Ireland, this list was initially twenty pages long, containing 67 bodies. Today, the list includes nearly 400 entities. Adjustments to the three lists have led to a rather wide range of public bodies; these entities are, however, connected to the executive power in some way.

The right of access to documents in Article 255 EC Treaty and Regulation 1049/2001 is applicable to documents held by the Commission, the European Parliament and the Council. In practice, many other bodies of the EU adhere to the provisions of Regulation 1049/2001. In the Constitutional Treaty, the scope of the right is broadened. If

---

11 See for instance Greece and Spain.

12 See Estonia, Finland, France, Hungary, Ireland, Italy, Lithuania, Poland, Portugal, the Slovak Republic and Sweden.

13 See for instance the Czech Republic and Estonia. In Denmark, the possibility of extending the scope to publicly funded entities is delegated to concerned ministers.

14 See for instance Lithuania.

15 See for instance Finland.

16 See for instance Estonia.

the Treaty becomes law, the right will apply to documents held by the Union institutions, bodies, offices and agencies.

Other Features

Finland and the Czech Republic distinguish between information that has entered the public domain ('already disclosed information') and documents that have not. Consequently, in the Czech Republic, when an authority receives an application for access to already disclosed information, the authority can simply provide the applicant with information on how to access the information. If however, the applicant insists on receiving the requested information directly, the authority is obliged to provide it. In Finland, rules on access to documents relate firstly to documents in the public domain. Documents that are not yet in the public domain are disclosed at the public authority's discretion.[17]

Czech and Slovak laws distinguish between 'disclosed information' on the one hand, and 'accompanying' or 'associated information' on the other. The first kind of information is always accessible. The second is information that is closely related to the requested information. Information also includes knowledge of the mere existence of the requested information, its origin or number, and also of the reasons for denial of access and the period of denial. Although not explicitly stated, it seems likely that this second form of information must always be given to an applicant. An exception exists where the protection of a certain interest requires absolute secrecy, and the accompanying information itself would reveal details of the substance of the requested information.

§ 6 Exceptions

Preliminary Remark

Before describing possible exceptions to access to documents, we first want to state that it is not always possible to draw a clear distinction between the *scope* of national legislation on access to documents, as described above, and *the exceptions to* these rules. This is especially the case when exceptions have a mandatory and absolute character, which means that public authorities *shall* deny access to a document when the exception applies (see below). A possible consequence of this distinction is the way in which public authorities have to answer a request for information. It seems likely that when a document falls outside the scope of the law, the public authority may end the process by simply communicating this fact to the applicant. While if the document is covered by an exception, the national law may require that public authorities give reasons for their denial. Another consequence concerns the possibility of administrative appeal and/or judicial review. In most cases it seems unlikely

[17] On the distinction between active and passive disclosure of information we refer to § 10.

that a denial of access to documents based on the fact that the document falls outside the scope of national legislation can be challenged. Being aware of these consequences, the distinction that is generally found in Member State law is followed below.

General Features

Many acts on access to documents contain *mandatory* and *discretionary* exceptions. If a document is covered by a 'mandatory' restriction, an authority must refuse access. Mandatory restrictions are usually formulated as 'access *shall* be denied'. 'Discretionary' restrictions leave it to the discretion of the authority to decide whether information will or will not be disclosed. These restrictions are formulated using the words 'may' or 'can'. Another distinction can be drawn between *absolute* and *relative* restrictions. Documents whose access is 'absolutely' restricted are *unconditionally* inaccessible, which is of course only possible in combination with mandatory restrictions. 'Relative' restrictions require that certain conditions be fulfilled before access is granted. This relative character can be given to mandatory as well as to discretionary exceptions. In general, one can distinguish between three relativity clauses: the harm test, a balancing of interests and the requirement of approval.[18]

The *harm test* implies that access shall or may be restricted when disclosure would be harmful to certain interests. The harm test appears in different wording and degree in national legislation. With regard to the wording, formulations used are 'damage', 'prejudice', 'jeopardise', 'injure', 'compromise', 'endanger', 'cause detriment' or 'have an adverse effect'. The degree of the test differs depending on the wording used in the national legislation. In some acts, access shall or may be denied when disclosure *could* harm a certain interest;[19] in other acts, access shall or may be denied when disclosure *would* harm a certain interest.[20] In other regulations, the test seems to be stricter. In Austria, an interest may not be *seriously* prejudiced and in Poland only where there is *substantial damage* to certain interests shall access be denied. Additional requirements can be found in Ireland, where disclosure shall or may in some cases be refused if it is *reasonably expected* or *would be likely* to harm a certain interest.

The second relativity clause, the balancing of interests, implies that a public authority has to balance the general interest of transparency and the interest protected by the exception. Only when the latter outweighs the former, access shall or may be denied.[21] Mostly, a formulation is used like 'when the interest of transparency is outweighed by any of the following interests...'.

---

[18] In addition, Denmark and Sweden make use of a kind of necessity test, which requires that access be denied only when secrecy is essential or necessary for the protection of certain interests.

[19] See for instance the Czech Republic.

[20] See for instance Hungary.

[21] See for instance Belgium, Greece, Ireland and the Netherlands.

The requirement of approval means that access to certain documents will only be granted when a person, company or other entity explicitly approves access. An example is access to documents containing personal data. Some countries require prior approval from the person concerned.[22] This is not the case in all countries; some make accessibility of documents containing personal data subject to a harm test or a balancing of interests.[23] In addition, some countries formulate access to personal data as a mandatory and absolute exception, whereas others place these documents outside the scope of general rules on access to documents.

Regulation 1049/2001 does not contain any absolute or discretionary exceptions. All exceptions are formulated as mandatory exceptions using the wording: 'institutions shall refuse access to a document where...'. These mandatory exceptions are of a relative nature. Three types of exceptions can be distinguished. The first category of exceptions is subject to a harm test: 'where disclosure would undermine the protection of...'. The second category is likewise subject to a harm test, but also to a balance test. Documents will still be disclosed if there is an overriding public interest in disclosure. The overriding public interest must be, according to the CFI, something more than the 'normal' public interest in disclosure of information. The third category is comparable with the second, albeit this category is subject to a stricter harm test: 'if disclosure would seriously undermine...'.

Secrecy Acts

In this analysis, it is not our ambition to summarise all the grounds on which access in a given Member State can or shall be denied. We refrain from doing so because of the wide variety of national rules in this respect and the limited nature of this survey. We will only discuss Secrecy Acts. For more in-depth information, we refer you to the EU and Member State survey in Part III.

Most Member States have some sort of Secrecy Act.[24] These acts apply to information whose disclosure is considered harmful to fundamental interests of the state. These interests include national security, defence and the territorial integrity of the state. These acts generally fulfil the requirements of international information security agreements, for instance, within the context of (accession to) NATO. These acts contain certain general features. Firstly, documents labelled as 'state secret' or 'restricted' (or some other wording) fall either outside the scope of the general law on access to documents[25] or are considered

---

[22] See the Czech Republic, Ireland and the Slovak Republic.

[23] See for instance some *Länder* in Germany and also the new Federal Information Act of Germany.

[24] English versions of these acts were found with regard to the Czech Republic, Estonia, Finland, Hungary, Ireland, Italy, Latvia, Lithuania, Poland, Portugal, the Slovak Republic, Slovenia and Sweden. At this point, we would like to recall the discussions at the EU level surrounding the well-known 'Solana'-decision that resulted in Article 9 of Directive 1049/2001.

[25] See for instance Estonia.

to be mandatory exceptions having an absolute character.[26] Secondly, according to the Secrecy Acts, classified documents are inaccessible to the general public. Thirdly, individuals may only access such information if they have a special permit, which is only issued after a security clearance. A person applying for a permit must show an interest and in most cases must be a citizen of the state concerned.[27] Fourthly, employees of public authorities who are competent to deal with this information can be prosecuted when the information is disclosed contrary to the rules of the Secrecy Act. Fifthly, the power to classify documents is granted to certain authorised persons or to a special Commission.[28]

In some countries, classification of a document is subject to time limits. In Portugal, for instance, the term of secrecy can be set for a maximum of four years, which can be extended by another four years if the reasons for secrecy still apply. In Sweden, the time limit can vary from two to seventy years, depending on the protected interest. In Hungary, a distinction is drawn between 'state secrets' and 'official secrets'. One of the consequences of this distinction is that documents belonging to the first category can be kept secret for a maximum of ninety years, whereas documents labelled 'official secrets' can be kept secret for a maximum of twenty years.

It is not always clear whether the legal remedies provided for in national law on access to information (see below) are also applicable to the decisions of public authorities concerning documents covered by the Secrecy Acts. The range of protected interests may sometimes be formulated in a broad way. For instance, in the Czech Republic, documents relating to important economic and political interests, rights and liberties of natural and legal persons and to the life and health of natural persons can under certain conditions also be classified.

Regulation 1049/2001 contains a separate regime for sensitive documents. The regime is further specified in the internal rules of the institutions. It is explicitly stated that these rules were formed without prejudice to Article 255 EC Treaty and Regulation 1049/2001. After an agreement between the EU and NATO was reached in 2003, the internal rules were amended. Access to classified information is given in accordance with the need-to-know principle. Authorisation of a person is done by the issuing of a security certificate. The legal remedies discussed below appear to be available to applicants.

Other Features

In addition to refusing access on substantive grounds, some countries may deny access on specific procedural grounds. The information acts of Ireland, Latvia and Slovenia contain detailed procedural requirements that individu-

---

[26] See for instance Italy.

[27] See for instance Estonia.

[28] An example of the latter can be found in Lithuania.

als must fulfil when applying for access to documents (see below). Failure to comply with these requirements can or shall lead to refusal of the application. In Belgium, a request will be denied when it is obviously formulated too vaguely. In some countries, access can be denied when the request seems obviously unreasonable or when the request is vexatious.[29] In Sweden, a public authority's obligation to disclose a document can cease to exist when the disclosure presents serious difficulties for the authority.

In a majority of countries, public authorities must grant partial access to documents if only some parts of a document are covered by an exception.[30]

Regulation 1049/2001 does not contain any procedural grounds for denial other than a failure to hand in an application within the set time-limits. If an application is not sufficiently precise the institution must ask the applicant to clarify the application. If the application relates to a very large number of documents, the institution concerned may confer with the applicant informally with a view to finding a fair solution. According to the case-law of the CFI, where a fair solution cannot be found, the institution is not allowed to simply deny disclosure of the documents on this ground.

If a requested document is only partly covered by one of the exceptions, the remaining parts of the document must be released.

---

§ 7 Procedural Requirements

With Regard to the Applicant

First, a few remarks must be made with regard to the difference between access to information and access to documents. It clearly makes a difference if one can simply ask for information concerning a certain matter, or if individuals must indicate the documents they want to access. In this respect, it is not easy to find common features in Member State law. It all depends on how an individual's right is formulated, how 'information' or 'document' is defined and how the conditions for making an application are described. However, if we nevertheless have to make some general remarks, we would conclude that according to most national information acts, applications have to contain a description, as detailed as possible, of the matter concerned and, where possible, a specification of the relevant documents. An exception can be found in Portugal, where requests for access must contain all references necessary for identifying the document. Only the Lithuanian Information Law explicitly distinguishes between information on the one hand and official documents on the other. The consequence of this distinction is that a request for access to official

---

29 See Belgium respectively Austria, Ireland and the United Kingdom.

30 See for instance the Czech Republic, Denmark and Ireland.

documents must be made in writing, while a request for access to information can be made orally.

In most countries, applications can be done orally or in writing. In Belgium, Portugal, the United Kingdom and with regard to official documents in Lithuania, a request must be made in writing.

National legislation differs in regard to what an application must contain. Examples of detailed requirements can be found in the national laws of Estonia, Ireland, Latvia, Portugal and Slovenia. In Latvia, for example, applicants are required to give their name and surname, domicile or place of residence in Latvia and their signature. In the case of restricted access information (see above), applicants have to state reasons and specify the purpose for which the information will be used. In Ireland and Slovenia, the applicant may specify the form or manner of access. The only country that explicitly allows an anonymous application is Finland.

In most countries, the public authority can, when granting access, require that the applicant pay a fee that may not exceed actual costs incurred by the public authority. In order to combat abuse of access rules, the Irish FOIA was amended to make it possible for an authority to demand an application fee that *can* exceed the authority's actual costs in producing the document. Applications can be denied or answers postponed so long as the applicant has not paid the fee. Similar rules apply in the United Kingdom.

Lastly, a remarkable feature can be found in Berlin's Information Act which explicitly prohibits using acquired information for commercial purposes.

A request for access to a document held by one of the three largest EU institutions must be made in writing. The application must be sufficiently precise in order to enable the institution to identify the document. Applicants are not obliged to state reasons for their request.

With Regard to the Public Authority

Almost all the national laws on access to documents set time limits within which public authorities have to answer requests for access. These limits vary from five working days (Estonia) to eight weeks (Austria). When reasons justify doing so, this period can generally be prolonged by another fixed period.[31] Almost half of the countries explicitly state that apart from the time limit, the request must be dealt with 'as soon as possible', with 'undue delay', 'immediately' or 'promptly'.[32] Some countries apply different time limits for the granting of access and the denial of access. In Hungary, for instance, the granting of access must be done within fifteen days, while a denial must be communicated to the applicant within eight days.

---

[31] In Austria, the possibility of prolonging is not subject to a time restriction.

[32] See respectively Denmark, Poland, Slovenia and the United Kingdom.

In practice, it often happens that an applicant sends his or her application to the wrong authority. Some countries regulate the manner in which an authority must confront this situation. Two possibilities exist: either the applicant must be informed of the error and the right authority must be indicated[33], or the application is forwarded to the proper authority.[34] In the case of the latter, the authority is often required to inform the applicant of the transferral. If the application is incomplete, sometimes the public authority is obliged to request additional information.[35] In Estonia, the authority has a general obligation to assist the applicant in every way and in the United Kingdom public authorities are obliged to provide advice and assistance.

Access to information in general means the possibility to immediately consult a document, obtain the original or a copy or extract of the document. Consultation or copying of the original document is sometimes made subject to the requirement that it will not damage the document.[36]

Most countries do not require that information be transmitted in a specific form. In the United Kingdom, public authorities must consider an applicant's preference of form, but only so far as is reasonably practicable. In Poland, information must be given in the form that the applicant requested, unless technical difficulties prevent the authority from doing so. In Sweden, an authority cannot be forced to disclose material recorded for automatic data processing in any other form than a printout.

Generally speaking, a decision to refuse access must be done in writing and some countries explicitly require public authorities to explain the reasons for denial.[37] In Latvia, a notification denying access to information must also contain possible remedies that the applicant can invoke.

According to Regulation 1049/2001, applications for access to a document shall be dealt with promptly. Access should either be granted or refused within 15 working days. A refusal must be made through a written reply that states reasons for the refusal. Access shall be provided for by way of consultation on the spot or by providing a copy of the requested document. The documents shall be supplied in an existing version and format with full regard to the applicant's preference.

---

33 See the Czech Republic and Latvia.

34 See Estonia, some *Länder* of Germany, the Netherlands and the Slovak Republic.

35 See for instance the Czech Republic and the Slovak Republic.

36 See France and Greece.

37 See amongst others France, Italy and Slovenia.

§ 8 Legal Remedies

As a preliminary remark, this study has focused on possible legal remedies provided for directly by national laws that concern access to information. This study did not review general administrative legislation. As was mentioned above, it is sometimes unclear whether legal remedies are available with regard to information falling within the scope of Secrecy Acts.

In general, Member State laws on access to documents contain three types of review procedures. Firstly, applicants may have the possibility of an *administrative* appeal. This appeal is generally lodged with the entity superior to the authority that refused access. In a few countries, the same authority will review a request that has been denied. Secondly, in some countries, applicants can file a complaint against denial of access with a supervisory Committee or Commissioner, whose purpose is to supervise the implementation of the rules on access to documents.[38] Thirdly, applicants can ask for *judicial* review by lodging an appeal to an administrative court. One of these legal remedies, a combination of two or all three of them can be found in almost all national legislation.

In the Czech Republic, applicants may appeal to an entity that is superior to the original authority. The decision of this superior entity cannot be judicially appealed. It appears that the Czech Republic is the only country that does not provide for judicial review. Some countries only allow for a possibility of judicial review.[39] The substantial majority of countries use a combination of one or all three review procedures.

Eight countries have some sort of supervisory Committee or Commissioner concerned with access to information (see in general below).[40] The role of these authorities differs from state to state. In Italy, the Committee on Access to Administrative Documents seems to have no competence with regard to individual cases where access has been denied. In Portugal, before making an administrative appeal, an applicant can ask for assistance from the Committee of Access to Administrative Documents. This Committee draws up a report on the issue and sends a copy to both the authority and applicant. After receiving the report, the authority will review its decision. In Belgium, an administrative appeal is combined with a request for the opinion of the Commission for Access to Administrative Documents. Within thirty days, the Commission sends an opinion on the matter to both the authority and applicant. The authority is not bound by the opinion of the Commission. In France, an applicant is obliged to

---

38 Generally, the national Ombudsman also has competence within the field of access to information. Its decisions, however, always have a non-binding nature. In this analysis, we restrict ourselves to describing the authorities specially equipped with the task of supervision in the field of access to information.

39 See for instance Finland and Sweden.

40 Besides these eight countries, Lithuania has a general Administrative Disputes Commission and four German *Länder* have appointed a Commissioner for Data Protection and Access to information.

submit a complaint to the Committee of Access to Administrative Documents before lodging an appeal in an administrative court. The Committee can issue a recommendation, which is not legally binding. On the other hand, in Hungary, the Data Protection Commissioner may instruct an authority to change or annul its negative decision. This order is legally binding; the authority may challenge it before a court. The same applies to the Information Commissioner in Ireland and the Commissioner on Access to Information of Public Character in Slovenia. In the United Kingdom, in principle, the Information Commissioner can issue a legally binding 'enforcement notice', which specifies the steps that an authority must take in order to fulfil the requirements of the Information Act. If the authority concerned does not comply with this notice, the Commissioner can bring the case before a court. The Commissioner's notice may also be subject to appeal to the Information Tribunal, after which, appeal on points of law is possible to the High Court of Justice.

It is not always clear whether the administrative court can order documents to be disclosed; only Hungary explicitly provides for this possibility.

A remarkable feature of the Slovenian Information Act is the possibility of fining a public authority employee when he or she is responsible for failing to disclose requested information within the set time limit. Some other countries provide for this possibility in their criminal laws.[41]

Finally, at least in Hungary and probably in Estonia, an applicant has legal remedies not only stemming from general access to documents but also regarding documents covered by Secrecy Acts.

If access is refused by one of the EU institutions, applicants have two remedies at their disposal. They can institute court proceedings at the CFI in order to have the negative decision annulled (Article 230 EC Treaty). Neither the CFI nor the ECJ have competence to order the institutions to publicly disclose a requested document. They can, however, order that the document be handed over to the Court, with a view to controlling whether the exception relied upon was justified. The second remedy is the ability to submit a complaint to the European Ombudsman under the conditions of Article 195 EC Treaty. The opinions of the Ombudsman are not binding on the institutions.

---

§ 9 Institutional Structure

In addition to the competences with regard to individual complaints as described above, most national supervisory authorities have broader competences in the field of access to documents. In general, these authorities are entrusted with supervising compliance with the national act on access to information. In this regard, they issue the above-mentioned opinions, recom-

---

41 See for instance Hungary and the Slovak Republic.

mendations and enforcement notices *on their own motion*. Some authorities are also entrusted with the task of promoting active publication of documents of relevance to the general public.[42] Most authorities must publish an annual report in which they explain their activities and describe general compliance with information rules by the public authorities.

In Hungary, public authorities have to annually report their denials of access to information to the Data Protection Commissioner. In Italy, the Committee on Access to Administrative Documents can propose amendments to Italian legislation on access to documents.

No special supervisory body exists with regard to Regulation 1049/2001, although Article 15 provides for an inter-institutional committee. The task of this committee is, however, limited to examining best practices, addressing possible conflicts and discussing future developments on public access to documents. On its own initiative, the ombudsman has taken several initiatives in the field of public access to documents. The EU institutions must annually publish a report regarding the preceding year.

---

§ 10 Other Characteristics

Passive versus Active Disclosure

In many of the national information acts, provisions are devoted to the *active* disclosure of information. This form of disclosure must be distinguished from *passive* disclosure, which refers to publication of information upon request. Some laws contain categories of documents the disclosure of which is mandatory (see above). Generally, public authorities are, within their sphere of competence, obligated to inform the public on matters of public interest. In Hungary, public authorities have to publish or otherwise enable access to the most important information concerning their activities. In Lithuania, public authorities must prepare and publish information concerning their functions, structure and current issues. In the Netherlands, an authority must disclose information on its own accord if such disclosure is 'in the interest of effective, democratic governance'. In Finland, public entities have the duty to promote access and good practices in information management. The latter concerns the quality of information and is regulated in more detail by separate legislation. The Polish Information Act is a mixture of provisions on active and passive disclosure of information. In accordance with this act, a Public Information Bulletin was created that discloses information to the general public. Slovak legislation requires that information be disclosed through 'mass access', meaning via telecommunications, especially the Internet. Similarly, Slovenia requires that information of public character be transmitted on the World Wide Web.

---

[42] See for instance Ireland.

Registers

In order to inform people about the information or documents that public authorities possess, some countries oblige authorities to maintain a register of documents.[43] Requirements with regard to the details of the information or documents are seldom provided for. In Latvia, authorities have to set out the class, designation and source of the information.

The EU institutions must as far as possible make documents directly accessible to the public in electronic form or through a register. This must in particular be done with regard to legislative documents. If direct access is not given through the register, the register must indicate where the document is located. Sensitive documents are only recorded in the register upon the consent of the originator.

---

§ 11 Concluding Observations

Are there any General Differences between the 'Old' and the 'New' Member States?

It is difficult to draw general conclusions with regard to the differences between legislation on access to information in the old and the new Member States of the EU. Perhaps the only possible conclusion is that at a general level these laws are predominantly similar. Differences only occur at a detailed level of legislation; however, even then it is difficult to distinguish between the two groups of States. Let us conclude that a comparison is in itself very instructive.

Although there is no clear or real demarcation-line between the access to information-regimes of the old and new Member States, there is a distinct difference in the traditions of access to information legislation between the 25 Member States. During the EU Conference 'Transparency in Europe – II', the representative from Estonia, Mr. Tallo, presented an interesting overview of three distinct traditions.[44] A first tradition in access to information legislation is based on the Anglo-American tradition. This tradition is characterised by the concept that government is a necessary evil and an enduring threat to the liberty of citizens (the Leviathan-concept of government). This characteristic leaves its mark on access to information-regimes, which reflect explicit public mistrust of the government and which impose strict obligations on governments and grant enforceable rights to information. The hallmarks of this tradition can for instance be found in the USA freedom of information legislation. The second

---

[43] See for instance Latvia and Slovenia.

[44] For a more detailed account of the discussions during the EU Conference 'Transparency in Europe – II' see H.R. Kranenborg, P.J. Stolk, A. Tunovíc & W.J.M. Voermans (eds.), *Transparency in Europe II*, 2005, ISBN 90541 40925.

tradition is the Continental one. In this tradition, government is not as much a threat but a trusted authority (Père Goriot) and access to information reflects an implicit trust by not over-emphasizing governmental obligations to grant citizens the right to access. The model is exemplified by the access to information legislation of France and Germany. Mr. Tallo's third model is the Nordic model. In this model, government is not predominantly trusted or mistrusted per se but acts as a partner to society and citizens. Together government and society forge government policies on the basis of available information. The ensuing access to information legislation reflects the idea of informed trust. Access to information legislation of this brand is to be found in Sweden, Denmark and Estonia.

Is the EU More or Less Transparent then the 'Average' Member State?

It is difficult to compare EU transparency with the 'average' Member State. As we have stated before, our research on transparency in the Member States is based solely on national legislation. Of course, one has to assess the practical implementation of legislation in order to answer questions concerning the degree of transparency. Also, EC legislation is not based on one of the three traditions mentioned above. Elements of all three can be found in Regulation 1049/2001. However, if one imagines a list of the transparency legislation of the 25 Member States in increasing order of transparency, meaning that the first place is the least transparent regime and the 25th place the most transparent regime, and if we had to put EC legislation somewhere on this list, it would most certainly not be at the end or the beginning. It would probably fall somewhere in the middle.

Most certainly the level of transparency will increase if the Constitutional Treaty is ratified by all Member States. Article I-50 of the European Constitution increases the openness-regime by changing over to a full-scale and comprehensive regime of transparency. The requirement that EU-institutions meet in public is an especially strong potential cure for the democratic deficit. The problem of the democratic deficit is urgent and does currently threaten European cooperation and the Constitution. In almost every scenario, the cure of Article I-50 of the Constitution is nearly a decade away. For this reason, some participants at the EU Conference 'Transparency in Europe – II' made an eloquent case for pre-implementing Article I-50 at this very moment. Others argued that such a step would be too drastic. They noted that Regulation 1049/2001 only just now was taking effect and that it would be far better to watch the development of this regime before taking the quantum-leap forward to a new regime.

Because of negotiations on the level of transparency for the 'European government' and because of close cooperation on many fields within the framework of the European Union, EC legislation, national legislation and the three different traditions intersect. Member States learn lessons from other Member

States. It is uncertain whether this may lead to higher or lower levels of transparency at both the national and European level.

Conclusion

One could ask what is the most desirable level of transparency; or which legislative regime is most ideal. We are not able to provide the answers. Inspired by the various legislation, we can try to formulate an ideal matrix within which we think access to information can best be modelled. We have tried to do so and presented a matrix containing three essential notions during the EU Conference 'Transparency in Europe – II'. These notions were supported by the participants. We took the principle of the rule of law as our point of departure.

Our first notion is that under the rule of law, access to information must in one way or another be construed as *a right for individuals*, be it a positive right or be it (through the mirror situation) an authority's obligation to provide information. The exact status and carving out of this right within the constitutional and legal framework of a country is, in our view, not as much a question of law, but rather a question of (political) appreciation. However, we note that the discussion on the fundamental nature of the right to access information was invigorated by the Treaty establishing a Constitution for Europe, in which the right to access documents is referred to twice.

Secondly, as a requirement of the rule of law, exceptions to the right to access to information must be *provided for by law*. The individual must be able to know on which grounds an application for information can or will be denied.

Thirdly, we believe that the rule of law requires that an individual's right to access be *effective*, implying that the right is enforceable before an independent authority. In order to form a realistic opinion on the denial of access, this independent authority must have access to the contested information, in spite of secrecy, labels and mandatory or absolute restrictions. An independent authority must also be able to annul the decision of a public authority and in the ideal situation, must be able to order disclosure of the information.

PART III

EU & Member State Survey

European Union

Legislation on access to information

- Article 1 EU Treaty and Article 255 EC Treaty
- Regulation (EC) 1049/2001 of the European Parliament and of the Council of 30 May 2001 regarding public access to European Parliament, Council and Commission documents[1]
- Article 42 EU Charter of Fundamental Rights[2]

Scope

Article 1 EU Treaty states that in the European Union decisions are taken as openly as possible. Article 255 EC Treaty reads:

> 1. Any citizen of the Union, and any natural or legal person residing or having its registered office in a Member State, shall have a right of access to European Parliament, Council and Commission documents, subject to the principles and the conditions to be defined in accordance with paragraphs 2 and 3.
> 2. General principles and limits on grounds of public or private interest governing this right of access to documents shall be determined by the Council, acting in accordance with the procedure referred to in Article 251 within two years of the entry into force of the Treaty of Amsterdam.
> 3. Each institution referred to above shall elaborate in its own Rules of Procedure specific provisions regarding access to its documents.

Regulation 1049/2001 is based on this provision. There is much debate about whether access to documents constitutes a fundamental right in the EU. Applicants before the European courts have relied on the fundamental nature of access to documents and have argued that certain provisions of the regulation must conform with the right.[3] Although the ECJ acknowledges the importance of the public's right to access documents, it has never accepted this right as fundamental.[4] Legal scholars have also advocated for the fundamental nature of the right of access to documents.[5] When the Treaty establishing a constitution for Europe (Constitutional Treaty) will become law, the discourse about the

---

1 OJ 2001, L 145/43.

2 OJ 2000, C 364/1.

3 See for instance CFI 5 March 1997, *WWF UK v. Commission*, case T-105/95 [1997] ECR II-313 and CFI 7 June 1998, *Svenska Journalistförbundet v. Council*, case T-174/95 [1998] ECR II-2289.

4 See ECJ 20 April 1996, *Netherlands v. Council*, case C-58/94 [1996] ECR I-2169, § 35. See also ECJ 6 December 2001, *Council v. Hautala*, case C-353/99 P [2001] ECR I-9594 and the opinion in this case of AG Léger 10 July 2001, [2001] ECR I-9565.

5 See for example D. Curtin, *Citizens' fundamental right of access to EU information: an evolving digital passepartout?*, in CMLRv 2000, no. 37, pp. 7-41.

fundamental nature of the right to access documents can be closed.[6] Firstly, the EU Charter of Fundamental Rights will form an integral part of the constitution and will therefore be legally binding. Article 42 of the Charter – which will become Article II-102 of the Constitutional Treaty – includes the right to access to documents. Presently, the Charter is not legally binding, because it was only 'solemnly proclaimed' during the Nice summit in December 2000. Secondly, the equivalent of Article 255 EC-treaty will be Article I-50. Not only is the scope widened (see below), the place of the article is also significantly changed. Article 255 is placed in the fifth part of the EC-treaty titled 'institutions of the Community' and is placed under the heading 'provisions common to several institutions'. In the constitutional treaty, on the other hand, the equivalent article is placed in part I, the constitutional part of the treaty, under the heading 'the democratic life of the Union'.

As can be derived from Article 255, the right to access documents is restricted to documents held by the European Parliament, the Council and the Commission. In practice, however, most of the other institutions and bodies comply with the rules of Regulation 1049/2001. An important exception is the Court of Justice. In the Constitutional Treaty this practice is confirmed through broadening the scope of the right to documents held by 'Union institutions, bodies, offices and agencies'.[7] According to Article III-399 of the Constitutional Treaty, the Court of Justice is also subject to the provisions of Article I-50, albeit only with regard to documents related to the exercise of its administrative tasks. A document is any content whatever its medium (written on paper or stored in electronic form or as a sound, visual or audiovisual recording) concerning a matter relating to the policies, activities and decisions falling within the institution's sphere of responsibility (Article 3 sub a Reg. 1049/2001). The right to access is granted to any citizen of the Union, and any natural or legal person residing or having its registered office in a Member State (Article 2 § 1 Reg. 1049/2001). Article 2 § 2 allows the institutions to grant access to documents to any natural or legal person not residing or not having its registered office in a Member State; all three institutions used this possibility.[8]

Point of Departure

In principle, all documents of the institutions are accessible to the public. However, exceptions apply for the protection of certain public and private interests.[9] These exceptions are laid down in Regulation 1049/2001.

---

6 OJ 2004, C 310/1.

7 See Article I-50 § 3 and II-102 Constitutional Treaty.

8 See Decision 2001/840 of the Council (OJ 2001, L 313/40), Decision 2001/937 of the Commission (OJ 2001, L 345/94) and Decision of the European Parliament (OJ 2001, L 374/1).

9 See § 11 of the preamble of Regulation 1049/2001.

Exceptions

The main exceptions are listed in Article 4. This article does not contain any absolute or discretionary exceptions.[10] All exceptions are formulated as mandatory exceptions using the wording: 'institutions *shall* refuse access to a document where...'. These mandatory exceptions are of a relative nature. There are three types of exceptions. Firstly, there are mandatory exceptions that are subject to a harm test (Article 4 § 1). Access shall be denied where disclosure *would undermine* the protection of:

a) the public interest as regards:
  - public security,
  - defence and military matters,
  - international relations,
  - the financial, monetary or economic policy of the Community or a Member State;

b) privacy and the integrity of the individual, in particular in accordance with Community legislation regarding the protection of personal data.

Secondly, a set of interests is protected when disclosure would undermine the protection thereof, unless there is an overriding public interest in disclosure (Article 4 § 2). When the latter 'exception to the exception' applies, access to the requested documents can still be granted. Recently the Court of First Instance ruled that 'an overriding public interest' must be something more then the 'normal' public interest in disclosure of information.[11] Protected interests are:

- commercial interests of a natural or legal person, including intellectual property,
- court proceedings and legal advice,
- the purpose of inspections, investigations and audits.

The third type of exception concerns internal documents (Article 4 § 3). A stricter harm test applies to these documents. Access shall be denied to internal documents if disclosure would *seriously* undermine the institution's decision-making process. Like the second exception, it is subject to the same 'overriding public interest'-test. Once the decision to which the internal documents relate is made, the exception applies only to documents containing opinions for internal use as part of deliberations and preliminary consultation within the institution concerned.

Different rules apply to documents originating from third parties, within which the documents originating from the Member States take a special position. Once a request is directed to a third-party document, the institutions

---

10 See Part II, § 6 for a clarification of this distinction.

11 CFI 23 November 2004, *Turco v. Council*, case T-84/03, n.y.p., § 83.

must consult the third party with a view to assessing whether an exception as formulated in Article 4 § 1 or 2 applies (see Article 4 § 4). Member States are special kinds of third parties. They may request an institution not to disclose a document originating from that Member State without prior permission (Article 4 § 5). Once a Member States prohibits an institution from granting access to a certain document, the institution is bound by the decision of the Member State.[12] The institution does not have to state reasons for its refusal, other than that the relevant Member State did not agree with disclosure. With regard to documents originating form other third parties, or documents to which no prior agreement is requested by the Member States, the institution does not seem bound by third party or member state opinions. However, in practice, the institutions mostly follow this opinion.[13]

The exceptions only apply during the period in which protection is justified on the basis of the content of the document (Article 4 § 7). The maximum period is 30 years. This maximum period can be extended in the case of documents relating to privacy or commercial interests and in the case of so-called 'sensitive documents'.

If an application relates to a very long document or to a very large number of documents, the institution concerned may confer with the applicant informally, with a view to finding a fair solution (Article 6 § 3). Where a fair solution cannot be found, the institution may not simply deny access or limit the scope of the examination which it is normally required to carry out in response to a request for access.[14]

If only parts of the requested document are covered by any of the exceptions, the rest of the document must be released (Article 4 § 6).

Sensitive Documents

Regulation 1049/2001 contains a separate regime for sensitive documents (see Article 9). These are documents classified as 'TRÈS SECRET/TOP SECRET', 'SECRET' or 'CONFIDENTIEL' in accordance with the rules of the institution concerned. This separate regime exists for the protection of the essential interests of the European Union or of one or more of its Member States in the areas covered by Article 4 § 1(a), notably public security, defence and military matters. Requests for access to these documents are handled by explicitly authorised persons (Article 9 § 2). Internal rules can be found in Council Decision 2001/264 and Commission Decision 2001/844.[15] These decisions, containing detailed rules on security, are made without prejudice to Article 255

---

[12] See CFI 30 November 2004, *IFAW Internationaler Tierschutz-Fonds GmbH v. Commission*, case T-168/02, n.y.p., § 58.

[13] See p. 25 of the Report of the European Commission of 30 January 2004.

[14] CFI 13 April 2005, *Verein für Konsumenteninformation v. Commission*, case T-2/03, n.y.p., § 96.

[15] Council Decision 2001/264 of 19 March 2001 (OJ 2001, L 101/1) and Commission Decision 2001/844 of 29 November 2001 (OJ 2001, L 317/1).

EC Treaty and Regulation 1049/2001. The rules are not only directed towards the Council and the Commission but also to responsible security authorities of the Member States. The Council also makes use of decentralised agencies. The classification of documents in the rules on security differs slightly from the ones in Regulation 1049/2001. The rules distinguish between four categories: 'TRÈS SECRET UE/EU TOP SECRET', 'SECRET EU', 'CONFIDENTIEL EU' or 'RESTREINT UE'.[16] The first classification applies only to information the unauthorised disclosure of which could cause exceptionally grave prejudice to the essential interests of the EU or one or more of its Member States. The second label concerns information whose disclosure could seriously harm the essential interests of the EU or one or more of its Member States. Information is classified as 'CONFIDENTIEL EU' when unauthorised disclosure could harm the essential interests of the EU or one or more of its Member States. Finally, the fourth classification concerns information the unauthorised disclosure of which could be disadvantageous to the interests of the EU or one or more of its Member States.

Information is classified only when necessary.[17] Article 5, section III of the Council Decision stresses the importance of using classification correctly and sparlingly.[18] The originator of information is responsible for classifying a document.[19] Access to classified information is given in accordance with the need-to-know principle.[20] Only persons who need to know certain information in order to carry out their duties or missions are authorised to access the information. Within the Council, the determination of need to know rests within the General Secretariat, the EU decentralised agencies and with the Member State's service or department in which the person concerned is employed. Within the Commission, the responsibility for determining need to know rests with the department in which the person concerned is employed. Authorisation of a person is done by the issuing of a security certificate. Both the Council Decision and the Commission Decision also contain detailed rules on the preparation, distribution, transmission, storage and destruction of EU classified material.[21] In an appendix attached to both decisions, an overview is given of the classification terminlogy used in the different Member States. These appendici were amended after the signing of an agreement between the EU and NATO in March 2003.[22]

---

16 Section II § 1-4 Council Decision and Article 16.1 Commission Decision.

17 Section III § 1 Council Decision and Article 17.1 Commission Decision.

18 See also Article 17.2 Commission Decision.

19 Section III, § 2 Council Decision and Article 17.1 Commission Decision.

20 Section V Council Decision contains the rules on the need-to-know principle, as does Article 19 Commission Decision.

21 Section VII Council Decision and Article 21 Commission Decision.

22 See Council Decision 2004/194 of 10 February 2004 (OJ 2004, L 63/48) and Commission Decision 2005/94 of 3 February 2005 (OJ 2005, L 31/66).

Procedural Rules

Applications for access to a document must be made in any written form and must be sufficiently precise to enable the institution to identify the document (Article 6 § 1). Applicants do not have to state reasons for their request (Article 6 § 1). If an institution finds that an application is not sufficiently precise, it can ask the applicant for a clarification (Article 6 § 2). Where possible, the institution is obliged to assist the applicant in doing so. Applications should be dealt with promptly (Article 7 § 1). Institutions must send an acknowledgment of receipt. Within 15 working days either access must be granted and provided or a written reply must be given which contains reasons for the refusal. In exceptional cases, this time-limit can be extended by another 15 days (Article 7 § 3). Where access is refused, the applicant can, within 15 working days, make a confirmatory application asking the institution to reconsider its position (Article 7 § 2). The institution must give an answer within 15 working days stating reasons for the refusal and informing the applicant of available remedies (Article 8 § 1). If, with regard to the initial application, the institution does not reply within the prescribed time-limit, the applicant is allowed to make a confirmatory application (Article 7 § 4). If the failure to answer within the time-limit concerns a confirmatory application, such failure is considered to be a refusal of the request (Article 8 § 3).

Access shall be provided for by way of consultation on the spot or by providing a copy of the requested document. Costs may be charged, as long as they do not exceed the real costs of producing and sending the copies (Article 10 § 1). The documents shall be supplied in an existing version and format with full regard to the applicant's preference (Article 10 § 3).

Legal Remedies

If an applicant receives a negative answer to the confirmatory application two remedies are available. Firstly, the applicant can institute court proceedings against the institution under Article 230 EC Treaty, by which the Court of First Instance may annul the decision. Possible annulment by the CFI does not imply that access to the documents is automatically granted. It only means that the institution concerned must reconsider its answer. In order to give a well founded judgment, the Courts may inspect the contested documents. It is not clear whether the same applies to sensitive documents. Secondly, the applicant can make a complaint to the European Ombudsman under Article 195 EC Treaty. The opinions of the Ombudsman are not binding on the institutions.

Institutional Structure

No special supervisory body exists with regard to Regulation 1049/2001, although Article 15 provides for an inter-institutional committee. The task of this committee is, however, limited to examining best practices, addressing possible conflicts and discussing future developments in public access to documents. The committee was formed and began operating in March 2002. Besides this committee, the European Ombudsman must be mentioned. By its own initiative, the ombudsman has taken several initiatives in the field of public access to documents.[23]

Other Characteristics

According to Article 12 Regulation 1049/2001, the institutions must as far as possible make documents directly accessible to the public in electronic form or through a register. This must, subject to the provisions contained in Article 4 and 9, in particular be done with regard to legislative documents, *i.e.* documents drawn up or received in the course of procedures for the adoption of acts which are legally binding in or for the Member States (Article 12 § 2). If direct access is not given through the register, the register must indicate where the document is located (Article 12 § 4). Sensitive documents are only recorded in the register with the consent of the originator (Article 9 § 3).

Each institution must annually publish a report for the preceding year. Article 17 § 2 instructed the Commission to publish an evaluation report by 31 January 2004. On 20 January 2004 the report was duly published.[24]

Article 5 of the regulation contains a rule on access to documents that are in the hands of the Member States and which originate from one of the EU institutions. Unless it is clear that the document concerned shall or shall not be disclosed, the Member State must consult the relevant institution so as to not jeopardise the objectives of Regulation 1049/2001.

Other Activities in the Field of Transparency

The activities of the institutions in the field of transparency are scrutinised by different NGO's. See for example *Statewatch* or *Freedominfo.org.*[25]

---

[23] For example, at a very early stage and by its own initiative the enquiry of 20 December 1996, which led to the adoption of (internal) rules on access to documents by several other institutions of the EC apart from the Commission, the Council and the European Parliament. This enquiry, and others, can be found at the website of the European Ombudsman http://www.europarl.eu.int/ombudsman/home/en/default.htm.

[24] See the Report of the European Commission of 30 January 2004, *infra* Part I, § 3.

[25] The websites of these two NGO's are http://www.statewatch.org and http://www.freedominfo.org.

Austria

Legislation on Access to Information

- Article 20 § 3 and 4 of the Austrian Federal Constitutional Law (*Bundes-Verfassungsgesetz*)[26]
- Federal Framework Act on Information (*Auskunftspflicht-Grundsatzgesetz*), no. 286/1987 of 15 May 1987
- Federal Act on the duty to furnish information (*Auskunftspflichtgesetz*), no. 287/1987 of 15 May 1987[27]

Scope

Article 20 § 4 of the Austrian Federal Constitutional Law reads:

> (4) All functionaries entrusted with Federation, *Länder* and municipal administrative duties as well as the functionaries of other public law corporate bodies shall impart information about matters pertaining to their sphere of competence in so far as this does not conflict with a legal obligation to maintain secrecy; an onus on professional associations to supply information extends only to members of their respective organisations and this inasmuch as fulfilment of their statutory functions is not impeded. The detailed regulations are, as regards the Federal authorities and the self-administration to be settled by Federal law in respect of legislation and execution, the business of the Federation; as regards the *Länder* and municipal authorities and the self-administration to be settled by Land law in respect of the framework legislation, they are the business of the Federation while the implemental legislation and execution are Land business.

On the federal level, this article of the Federal Constitutional Law has led to the Federal Act on the duty to furnish information (the Federal Information Act, FIA). Anyone can ask for access to information (Article 2 FIA). Access to information is not formulated as a right for citizens or persons; rather, competent authorities have a duty *to answer requests* for information, in so far as such requests do not conflict with a legal obligation to maintain secrecy. Therefore, public authorities are not obliged to *impart* the requested information. The FIA applies to Federal authorities and self-administrative authorities appointed by federal act. The scope of 'information' (*'Auskunft'*) is not further clarified. Framework Act no. 286/1987 applies to the *Länder* and municipalities (*'Gemeinden'*). In Article 2 of the Act, the right to *ask* for information is granted to everyone (*'Jedermann hat das Recht, Auskünfte zu verlangen'*). Legislation passed by the *Länder* provides for detailed rules.[28]

---

[26] An English translation of the Federal Constitutional Law can be found at http://www.ris.bka.gv.at/info/bvg_eng.pdf.

[27] The German text of this Act can be found via http://www.ris.bka.gv.at/nol/.

[28] The German texts of these acts can be found via http://www.ris.bka.gv.at/nol/. In the following only the FIA will be discussed.

Point of Departure

Public authorities shall impart information in so far as this does not conflict with a legal obligation to maintain secrecy.

Exceptions

According to Article 20 § 3 of the Austrian Federal Constitutional Law, all functionaries entrusted with Federal, *Länder* and municipal administrative duties as well as the functionaries of other bodies created in accordance with public law are, save as otherwise provided by law, sworn to secrecy about all facts that they have obtained exclusively through their official activities. Such concealment may be justified in the interest of public peace, order and security, universal national defence, external relations, for the preparation of a ruling or as in the preponderant interest of the parties involved (official secrecy).

Information will be provided to the extent that it does not seriously prejudice the effective conduct of the public authority's duties (Article 1 § 2 FIA). Additionally, information is not distributed when the request has obvious abusive purposes (*'wenn sie offenbar mutwillig verlangt werden'*, Article 1 § 2 FIA).

If other federal acts contain special rules on the duty to provide information, they have precedence over the FIA (Article 6 FIA).

Procedural Rules

Applicants can make their request in writing or orally. If an oral request is unclear, the public authority can ask the applicant to restate their request in writing (Article 2 FIA). Public authorities are obligated to answer requests for information within eight weeks (Article 3 FIA). The applicant must be informed when, because of special circumstances, this time limit will be exceeded.

Legal Remedies

If information is not imparted, the applicant can ask for a formal answer (*'Bescheid'*) to his request (Article 4 FIA). An applicant may invoke the procedural rules laid down in the General Administrative Procedure Act, unless the requested information falls within the scope of another, more specific act.[29]

Institutional Structure

Access to documents is not overseen by special supervisory authorities.

---

[29] The German text of the General Administrative Procedure Act can be found at http://www.standesbeamte.at/download/AVG_1_10_2002.pdf.

Belgium

Legislation on Access to Information[30]

- Article 32 of the Belgium Constitution[31]
- On a federal level: Act no. 94-1724 of 11 April 1994 on the disclosure of information by the administration[32] and Federal Act of 12 November 1997 on the disclosure of information by the administration is applicable to provinces and municipalities[33]
- On a regional and community level there exist many decrees on access to documents: for instance the Flemish Decree of 27 March 2004, the Walloon Decrees of 30 March and 7 March 2001, the Decree of the French Community of 22 December 1994, the Ordonnance of the Brussels Region of 30 March 1995, the Decree of the French Community Commission of the Brussels Region of 11 July 1996, the Ordonnance of the Common Community Commission of the Brussels Region of 26 June 1997, the Decree of the German speaking Community of 16 October 1995[34]

Scope

Article 32 of the Belgium Constitution reads:

> Everyone has the right to consult any administrative document and to have a copy made, except in the cases and conditions stipulated by the laws, decrees or rulings referred to in Article 134.

The right to consult and make a copy of any administrative document is granted to everyone – including foreigners and legal persons. At the federal level, Article 32 is implemented by the Act of 11 April 1994 on the disclosure of information by the administration (the Federal Information Act, FIA). According to the FIA, 'administrative document' means any information, in whatever format, that is at an executive authority's disposal (Article 1b, sub 2). According to Article 1b,

[30] See for a survey (in Dutch) on legislation on access to official documents in Belgium: http://user.online.be/~fschram/013.htm. See in general F. Schram, *Executive transparency in Belgium*, in *Freedom of Information Review*, October 2001, p. 34-41, F. Schram, *Openbaarheid van bestuur* (Administratieve Rechtsbibliotheek – beknopt), Brugge, 2003 and P. de Hert, *De grondrechten en wetten m.b.t. openbaarheid van bestuursdocumenten en bescherming van de persoonlijke levenssfeer. Analyse van de onderlinge relatie en commentaar bij het arrest Dewinter van de Raad van State*, in *C.D.P.K.* 2001, pp. 374-425. The following survey concentrates only on the Federal Information Act.

[31] An English translation of the Belgium Constitution can be found at http://www.fed-parl.be/gwuk0002.htm.

[32] A French text of this Act can be found via http://www.juridat.be/cgi_loi/legislation.pl.

[33] A Dutch text of this Act can be found via http://users.online.be/~fschram/vind.html.

[34] Dutch texts of this Acts can be found via http://users.online.be/~fschram/vind.html.

sub 1, the meaning of 'administrative authority' is further specified in Article 14 of the Act on the Council of State, from which a broad notion can be extracted. The exact scope of this notion is subject to debate.[35] At the moment the Federal Information Act is in revision.

Point of Departure

Every administrative document is public unless one of the exceptions applies.[36]

Exceptions

Article 6 § 1 FIA contains mandatory exceptions that must be applied after a balancing of interests. Access shall be denied when the administrative authority finds that transparency is outweighed by any of the following interests:

- public safety
- the freedoms and fundamental rights of citizens
- the federal international relations of Belgium
- public order, police matters or national defence
- investigation and prosecution of punishable acts
- a federal economic or financial interest, the currency or public finance
- confidential business information or information on manufacturing processes communicated to the authority
- secrecy of the identity of the person who communicated the document or the information to the public authority on a confidential basis so as to denounce a punishable act or one presumed to be so.

The exceptions in Article 6 § 2 are obligatory after a harm test is applied. Access shall be denied if the disclosure of the requested information *prejudices*:

- personal privacy, unless the person concerned gives prior written authorisation to the consulting or copying of the document
- an obligation of secrecy established by law
- the secrecy of deliberations by the Federal Government and the Federal executive authorities or those associated with a Federal authority.

Article 6 § 3 contains optional exceptions that administrative authorities may invoke. Disclosure of a document may be rejected if the request:

- concerns an administrative document whose disclosure might be misunderstood because it is incomplete or not finalised

[35] See Schram (2001), p. 36.

[36] See de Hert (2001), p. 376.

- concerns a confidential opinion that is freely communicated to the authority
- is obviously unreasonable
- is obviously formulated too vaguely.

Procedural Rules

Requests for information must be made in writing (Article 5 FIA). The application should include the relevant issue, and, where possible, the relevant documents. The administrative authority must reply within a period of thirty days after receipt of the application (Article 6 § 5). A fifteen-day extension is possible and must be communicated to the applicant.

If part of a document does not fall within the scope of one of the exceptions, the administrative authority is obliged to make the document partially available (Article 6 § 4).

Legal Remedies

When access to information is denied, the applicant can, in accordance with Article 8 § 2 FIA, reapply and request an opinion from the Commission for Access to Administrative Documents (see below). The Commission has thirty days to issue its opinion, which it sends to the applicant and the administrative authority. The latter has another fifteen days to reply to the second request. The public authority's failure to decide upon the second request is considered a refusal. After this administrative appeal, the applicant can file a complaint with the Council of State (Article 8 § 2).

Institutional Structure

Article 8 § 1 FIA created the Commission for Access to Administrative Documents. The Commission has competence to issue an opinion on request of an individual, of an administrative authority or on its own motion. Since 1997, the Commission has had competence over provincial and municipal documents.[37]

Other Characteristics

Under the FIA, individuals have a right to correct any inaccurate information contained in administrative documents, provided that such information relates to the individual concerned (Article 7).

[37] See Schram (2001), p. 38.

Czech Republic

Legislation on Access to Information

- Article 17 of Law No. 2/1993, the Charter of Fundamental Rights and Freedoms.[38] According to Article 3 of the Constitution of the Czech Republic, this Charter forms an integral component of the country's constitutional system[39]
- Law No. 106/1999 Coll. on Free Access to Information of 11 May 1999[40]
- Law No. 148/1998 Coll., on the protection of Classified Information of 1998

Scope

Article 17 of the Charter, under the heading 'Political Rights', reads:

> (1) Freedom of expression and the right to information are guaranteed.
> ...
> (4) The freedom of expression and the right to seek and disseminate information may be limited by law in the case of measures essential in a democratic society for protecting the rights and freedoms of others, the security of the State, public security, public health, and morality.
> (5) Organs of the State and of local self-government shall provide in an appropriate manner information on their activity. The conditions and the form of implementation of this duty shall be set by law.

This article is further delineated in Law No. 106/1999 Coll. on free Access to Information (LAI). According to Article 3 § 1 LAI, 'applicant' means any natural or legal person requesting information. Instead of formulating access to information as a right granted to everyone, the LAI imposes a general obligation on state authorities to disclose all information in their sphere of competence, unless restrictions apply. Natural or legal persons mainly have a right to obtain access to already published information. If an application is for access to disclosed information, the public authority must inform the applicant how to obtain the information (Article 6 § 1). If an applicant insists on the direct distribution of

---

38 An English translation of the Charter can be found at http://www.psp.cz/cgi-bin/eng/docs/laws/listina.html.

39 The Constitutional Act No. 1/1993 Coll. of the Czech National Council of 16th December 1992 as amended by Acts No. 347/1997 Coll., 300/2000 Coll., 448/2001 Coll., 395/2001 Coll. and 515/2002 Coll. translated in English can be found at http://www.psp.cz/cgi-bin/eng/docs/laws/constitution.html.

40 Two diverging English translations can be found at http://www.env.cz/www/cenia.nsf/0/a19374a654a3f248c1256e270050d4f2?OpenDocument and http://home.online.no/~wkeim/files/foia-czech.htm, both translations are used.

published information, the responsible entity is obliged to provide it (Article 6 § 2).

State authorities are considered to be state bodies, self-administrative territorial bodies and public institutions financed through public funds (Article 2 § 1). These bodies are called 'responsible entities'. Entities consigned by law to make decisions on rights, lawfully protected interests, or obligations of natural or legal persons in the sphere of public administration are – in the scope of their decision making activity – also considered 'responsible entities' (Article 2 § 2).

The LAI draws a distinction between 'disclosed information' and 'accompanying information'. 'Disclosed information' means information that can be looked up and obtained, namely information published in print or in another format that can be recorded and stored, displayed in an official file, accessed remotely or housed in a public library (Article 3 § 3). 'Accompanying information' is information that is closely related to the requested information (Article 3 § 4).

Point of Departure

Concerned entities are obliged to actively (upon their own motion) disclose information, unless such information is, in accordance with legal regulations, labelled as secret or prohibited by provisions of the LAI.

Exceptions

The LAI contains a number of mandatory and absolute restrictions. Information labelled as 'secret' shall not be disclosed by the responsible entity (Article 7). Detailed rules are laid down in Law No. 148/1998 Coll., on the protection of Classified Information (LCI). According to Article 3 § 1 LCI, 'classified information' is information whose unauthorised disclosure could cause detriment to the interests of the Czech Republic or to those interests which the Czech Republic has undertaken to protect, or which could be unfavourable to these interests, and which is included in the register of classified information. According to Article 2 § 1 LCI, it is in the interest of the Czech Republic to preserve its constitutionality, sovereignty, territorial integrity, defence of the state, public safety, protection of important economic and political interests, rights and liberties of natural persons and legal entities and the life or health of natural persons. Four categories of security classification are distinguished: 'top secret', 'secret', 'confidential' and 'restricted' (Article 5 LCI). This classification plays an important role throughout the LCI. Access to classified information is only possible for persons for whom access is essential in order to carry out their activities and who fulfil certain conditions (Article 17 LCI). These conditions vary from being a citizen of the Czech Republic (Article 18 LCI) to being a person of suitable integrity (Article 20 LCI).

Another mandatory and absolute restriction is laid down in Article 9 LAI: information labelled as 'trade secrets' shall not be disclosed. This is further specified in section 17 of Law No. 513/1991 Coll., the Commercial Code.

Article 11 LAI contains both mandatory and discretionary restrictions. With regard to internal and preparatory documents:

> (1) A liable entity *may* restrict the provision of information if:
> a) it relates exclusively to the internal guidelines and staff regulations of the liable entity,
> b) new information is at issue that emerges in the preparation of a decision of the liable entity, unless the law stipulates otherwise; this applies only until such time as the preparation ends in a decision.

With regard to information originating from other persons or entities, responsible entities *shall* not provide information, unless the person consents (§ 2).

> (3) When providing information that a liable entity has obtained from a third party to fulfil tasks pursuant to a separate law, under which such information is subject to the obligation of confidentiality or other process protecting it from publication or abuse, but which can be provided under this Act, the liable entity shall provide only such information that relates directly to the fulfilment of its task.

Liable entities shall – according to § 4 – not provide information on:

> a) criminal proceedings in progress,
> b) the decision-making activities of courts,
> c) the fulfilment of the tasks of intelligence services,
> d) the preparation, course, and discussion of the results of inspections within the bodies of the Supreme Inspection Office,
> e) the activities of the respective organisational unit of the Ministry of Finance under a separate legal regulation.

The provisions of separate laws on the provision of information in the stipulated areas are not hereby affected.

The exception laid down in Article 8 LAI concerning protection of personal data and privacy was deleted after the adoption of Law No. 101/2000 Coll. on the Protection of Personal Data of 11 June 1998.[41] Now, according to Article 2 § 3 LAI, the LAI does not apply to the protection of personal data.

After applying the restrictions, a responsible entity is obliged to disclose the remaining information, including accompanying information (Article 12 LAI).

---

[41] An English translation of this Act can be found at http://www.nbu.cz/en/act148.php.

Procedural Rules

An application for access to information is submitted either in writing or orally (Article 13 § 1 LAI). If following an oral application the information is not disclosed or the applicant is of the opinion that the information provided for is insufficient, the application must be submitted in writing (Article 13 § 2).

If an application for access to already published information is made, the responsible entity must as soon as possible inform the applicant how to obtain the information; the entity must provide this information at the latest within seven days (Article 6 § 1). If the applicant insists on obtaining the information directly, an application has to be submitted. This application must include the applicant's name and must make clear to which responsible entity it is directed (Article 14 § 2). If an application is considered too vague, the responsible entity shall invite the applicant to clarify the request within seven days (Article 14 § 3a). If the application is sent to the wrong entity, the applicant shall be so informed within three days (Article 14 § 3b). If the application is valid, the responsible authority shall provide the requested information within fifteen days (Article 14 § 3c). For significant reasons, this time limit can be extended, maximally by ten days (Article 14 § 5).

Legal Remedies

The responsible entity must issue a decision if it fails to satisfy an application (Article 15 LAI). Within fifteen days, the applicant can lodge an appeal to the responsible entity (Article 16 § 1). The entity immediately superior to the responsible entity decides on the appeal (Article 16 § 2). No appeal can be lodged against this second decision (Article 16 § 4).

Institutional Structure

Access to documents is not overseen by special supervisory authorities.

Other Characteristics

According to Article 5 § 1g and 18 LAI, each responsible entity must publish an annual report on its activities in the provision of information under the LAI.

Denmark

Legislation on Access to Information

- The Danish Public Administration Act no. 571 of 19 December 1985[42]
- Act no. 572 of 19 December 1985 on Access to Public Administration Files as amended by Acts no. 347 of 6 June 1991, 504 of 30 June 1993, 276 of 13 May 1998 and 429 of 31 May 2000[43]

Scope

With regard to the broader concept of transparency, the Danish Constitution (*'Grundlov'*) states that meetings of the national parliament (*'Folketing'*) shall in principle be public (Article 49) and that in the administration of justice all proceedings shall to the widest possible extent be public (Article 65). However, the Danish Constitution does not contain any provisions on freedom of information or access to documents. Initially, the rules on public access to government information only concerned individuals – as interested parties.[44] Subsequently, the scope of this right broadened, but separate rules for interested parties still remained to exist. This history explains why access to documents in Denmark, since 1985, is found in two acts: the Danish Public Administration Act no. 571 (Act 571) and Act no. 572 on Access to Public Administration Files (Act 572). As this research focuses on access to documents based on public interest, the latter will be more closely examined.

Act 572 applies to all public administrative activities, except for matters relating to criminal justice (Articles 1 § 1 and 2 § 1). Matters relating to the making of laws are addressed in Act 572 (Article 2 § 2). According to Article 2, Act 572 also applies to any public utility generating, transmitting or distributing electricity at voltages of 500 volts or more; to natural gas suppliers and to any collective district heating plant falling under the Danish Heating Act and having a capacity of 10 MJ/s or more. By order, the concerned minister can, upon consultation with the Minister of Justice, provide that Act 572 also apply to entities that can not be classified as part of public administration, provided that the operating expenses of such entities are mainly covered by government funds or are statutorily empowered to make decisions on behalf of the government (Article 1 § 3).

---

42 A moderate English translation of this Act can be found at http://aabenhedskomite.homepage.dk/07love/forvaltningsloven_paa_engelsk.htm.

43 An English translation of this Act can be found at www.privacyinternational.org/countries/denmark/dk-foi-85.doc.

44 See L. Prakke & C.A.J.M. Kortmann, *Constitutional Law of the 15 EU Member States*, Deventer 2004, p. 855/6 and I. Österdahl, *Openness v. Secrecy: Public Acces to Documents in Sweden and the European Union*, in *E.L.Rev.* 1998, p. 176.

Article 4 § 1 Act 572 reads:

> Subject to the exceptions listed in Sections 7-14 of this Act, any person may demand that he be apprised of documents received or issued by an administration authority in the course of its activity. An administration authority may allow wider access to documents save where this is not allowed under the rules on secrecy etc.

According to Article 5 § 1, the right to access administrative files applies to all documents relating to the matter in question, including duplicate copies of letters issued by the authority concerned (where such letters are assumed to have reached the addressee), journal entries, registers, and other pertinent lists. Except for the latter records, the right of access to administrative files does not apply to registers or other systematic records processed electronically (Article 5 § 2).

With regard to different provisions of Act 572, the Act gives the minister concerned the competence to expand, reduce or further specify the scope of these provisions.

Point of Departure

All information shall be accessible, unless exceptions provided for by Act 572 apply.

Exceptions

Articles 7 and 8 Act 572 concern the right to access to internal case material. This right *shall not apply* to any document prepared by an authority for its own use; to correspondence between units within one and the same authority and to correspondence between a local government council and its committees departments and other bodies, or between these bodies (Article 7). However, the right of access to files shall comprise internal case material available in final form where such documents render exclusively the substance of the authority's final resolution on its decision in a matter; render exclusively information that the authority was bound to make a note of pursuant to the provision of Section 6 (see below) of Act 572; are self-contained instruments prepared by an authority for the purpose of producing evidence or clarity with respect to the facts of a matter; or contain general guidelines for the consideration of specified classes of matters (Article 8).

According to Article 10, the right of access *shall not apply* to records of meetings of the Council of State; minutes of meetings of ministers, and documents prepared by an authority for use at such meetings; correspondence between ministries relating to the making of laws, including Appropriation Bills; documents exchanged in connection with the secretarial function of one authority on behalf of another authority; correspondence between authorities and outside experts for use in court proceedings or in deliberations on possible legal proceedings; material gathered for the purpose of public statistics or scientific research.[45] If factual information mentioned in Article 10 – except for public statistics or scientific research materials – and Article 7 is of material importance to the matter in question, such information shall nevertheless be disclosed (Article 11).

The right of access to administrative documents shall not apply to personal data and information on technical plants or processes or on operating or business procedures or the like, provided it is of material importance to the economy of the person or enterprise that the request be refused (Article 12).

According to Article 13, the right of access to administrative files *may* be subject to limitations where protection is *essential* to:

1° the security of the State or the defence of the realm;
2° protection of Danish foreign policy or Danish external economic interests, including relations with foreign powers or international institutions;
3° prevention and clearing-up of any infringement of the law, prosecution of offenders, execution of sentences and the like, and protection of persons accused, of witnesses or others in matters of criminal or disciplinary prosecution;
4° implementation of public supervision, control, regulation, or planning activities, or of measures planned under taxation law;
5° protection of public financial interests, including interests relating to public commercial activities; or
6° protection of private or public interests where secrecy is required because of the special nature of the matter.

The duty to disclose information is limited by special provisions regarding secrecy laid down in specified legislation (Article 14).

Where the provisions of Article 12 and 13 apply to only part of a document, the person requesting disclosure shall be apprised of the rest of the contents of that document (Article 12 § 2 and 13 § 2).

Procedural Rules

A request for information shall specify the documents or the matter that the applicant wants to be apprised of (Article 4 § 3 Act 572). The authority deciding upon the issue concerning the requested matter shall give a reply to the application, or else the request shall be dealt with by the administrative authority possessing the document (Article 15 § 1). The authority shall decide upon the request as soon as possible (Article 16 § 1). Where a decision has not been made

45 An exception for documents prepared in connection with consideration of proposals for adoption by the EC or relating to interpretation and construction of or compliance with EC-rules, was deleted.

within ten days of receipt of the application, the relevant authority shall inform the person requesting disclosure of the reason why and of the date when a decision may be expected (Article 16 § 2).

Legal Remedies

According to Article 15 § 2 Act 572, a 'separate appeal shall lie to the authority otherwise empowered to hear appeals from the consideration given to or the decision made in the matter to which the request for disclosure is related'. The minister concerned may 'by Order' lay down rules derogating from the provisions laid down in Article 15 § 1 and 2 (Article 15 § 3).

Institutional Structure

Access to documents is not overseen by special supervisory authorities.

Other Characteristics

Under Article 6 § 1 Act 572, administrative authorities have the special duty to take notes:

> In any matter to be decided by an administration authority, an authority receiving information by word of mouth on facts of importance to the decision or in other manner having notice of such facts, shall make a note of the substance of such information, always provided that such information is not contained in the documents of the matter.

Estonia

Legislation on Access to Information

- Article 44 of the Estonian Constitution of 28 June 1992[46]
- Public Information Act of 15 November 2000, RT I 2000, 92, 597[47]
- State Secrets Act of 26 January 1999, RT I 1999, 16, 271[48]

Scope

Article 44, the right to information, of the Estonian Constitution reads:

> (1) Everyone shall have the right to freely receive information circulated for general use.
> (2) At the request of Estonian citizens, and to the extent and in accordance with procedures determined by law, all state and local government authorities and their officials shall be obligated to provide information on their work, with the exception of information which is forbidden by law to be divulged, and information which is intended for internal use only.
> (3) Estonian citizens shall have the right to become acquainted with information about themselves held by state and local government authorities and in state and local government archives, in accordance with procedures determined by law. This right may be restricted by law in order to protect the rights and liberties of other persons, and the secrecy of children's ancestry, as well as to prevent a crime, or in the interests of apprehending a criminal or to clarify the truth for a court case.
> (4) Unless otherwise determined by law, the rights specified in Paragraphs (2) and (3) shall exist equally for Estonian citizens and citizens of other states and stateless persons who are present in Estonia.

As this article makes clear, the right to access to documents applies to everyone in the territory of Estonia. Paragraph 2 has led to the Public Information Act (PIA). The PIA contains very detailed rules on access to public information. Only the main characteristics will be discussed below.

According to Article 3 § 1 PIA 'public information' means information which is recorded and documented in any manner and on any medium and which is obtained or created upon performance of public duties provided by law or legislation issued on the basis thereof. Holders of information are state and local government agencies and legal persons in public law (Article 5 § 1). The obligations of these public authorities extend to legal persons in private law and natural persons if the persons perform public duties pursuant to law, admin-

46 An English translation of the Estonian Constitution can be found at http://www.oefre.unibe.ch/law/icl/en00000_.html.

47 An English translation of this Act can be found at http://www.legaltext.ee/text/en/X40095K2.htm.

48 An English translation of this Act can be found at http://www.legaltext.ee/text/en/X30057K6.htm.

istrative legislation or contracts, including the provision of educational, health care, social or other public services, – with regard to information concerning the performance of their duties (Article 5 § 2). Equal to public authorities are companies which have a dominant position in the market or have special or exclusive rights or which are natural monopolies – with regard to information concerning the conditions and prices of the supply of goods and services and changes thereto, and non-profit associations, foundations and companies of which the state, a local government or a legal person in private law is a member or the founder or in which the state, a local government or a legal person in private law is a participant, – with regard to information concerning the use of funds allocated from the state or a local government budget (Article 5 § 3).

Article 2 § 2 states that information classified as a state secret falls outside the scope of the PIA. The same applies to information subject to special rules concerning access as laid down in specific legislation, for example the Archive Act or international agreements. Access to state secrets is addressed in the State Secrets Act, which will be discussed below.

The PIA distinguishes between access to information on the basis of requests for information (chapter 3) and disclosure of information on individual motion (chapter 4). With regard to the latter, Article 28 PIA contains a detailed list of information that must be disclosed.

Point of Departure

Every person has access to information *intended for public use* under the conditions and pursuant to the procedure provided by law (Articles 1 and 3 § 1 PIA).

Exceptions

According to Article 34 PIA, a public authority *may* classify information as 'internal'. Article 35 provides eleven cases in which an authority is *required* to classify information as intended for internal use:

1) information collected in criminal or misdemeanour proceedings until the case is referred to a court but not for longer than until end of the limitation period;
2) information collected in the course of state supervision proceedings until the entry into force of a decision made thereon;
3) information the disclosure of which would damage the foreign relations of the state;
4) information on the armaments and location of military units and personnel of the Defence Forces, unless this information is a state secret;
5) information the disclosure of which would endanger objects protected under heritage conservation;
6) information the disclosure of which would endanger the preservation of protected areas or protected species or varieties and their habitats;

7) information including a description of security systems, security organisations or security measures;
8) information on technological solutions if disclosure of such information would damage the interests of the authority concerned or if classification of such information as internal is prescribed in a contract entered into with a person in private law;
9) any other information provided by law;
10) information which contains private or sensitive personal data;
11) information which contains personal data if it significantly breaches the inviolability of private life of the data subject.

The head of a state, a local government agency or a legal person in public law *may* classify the following as information intended for internal use:

1) draft legislation of general application before it is sent for approval or presented for passage;
2) draft administrative legislation of specific application and its accompanying documents before passage or signature of the administrative legislation;
3) in justified cases, documents addressed to persons within the agency which are not registered in the document register (opinions, notices, memoranda, certificates, advice, etc.).

A state, local government agency or a legal person in public law shall not classify the following as information intended for internal use (Article 36):

1) results of public opinion polls;
2) generalised statistical surveys;
3) economic and social forecasts;
4) notices concerning the state of the environment;
5) reports on the work or the work-related success of the holder of information and information on the quality of the performance of duties and on managerial errors;
6) information which damages the reputation of a state or local government official, a legal person in private law performing public duties or a natural person, except sensitive or private personal data;
7) information on the quality of goods and services arising from protection of the interests of consumers;
8) results of research or analyses conducted by the state or local governments or ordered thereby, unless disclosure of such information would endanger national defence or national security;
9) documents concerning the use of budgetary funds of the state, local governments or legal persons in public law and remuneration and compensation paid from the budget;

10) information concerning the proprietary obligations of the holder of information;
11) information on the property of the holder of information;
12) precepts which have entered into force and legislation which is issued by way of state supervision or supervisory control or under disciplinary procedure and information relating to punishments in force.

This prohibition also applies to:

1) non-profit associations, foundations or companies which are founded by the state, local governments or legal persons in public law or in which the state, local governments or legal persons in public law participate;
2) information pertaining to the use of funds allocated and assets transferred to legal persons in private law from the state or a local government budget.

According to Article 38 § 4, the head of an agency may decide to grant access to internal information to persons outside the agency if this does not damage the interests of the state or local government. If the grant of access to information may cause the disclosure of restricted information, it shall be ensured that only the part of the information or document to which restrictions on access do not apply may be accessed (Article 38 § 2). According to Article 42, a public authority is required to invalidate a restriction on access if the reasons for the restriction cease to exist.

State Secrets Act (SSA)

State secrets are divided into four different categories: 'restricted', 'confidential', 'secret' and 'top secret' (Article 3 SSA), pursuant to the importance of secrecy. Detailed rules are laid down on what information falls within each category (Articles 4-7 SSA). State secrets are protected from disclosure in *the interest of the national security* (Article 2 § 1 SSA). Access to state secrets can only be obtained by virtue of a person's office, on the basis of a permit for access, by order of a preliminary investigator or prosecutor or on the basis of a court ruling (Article 22 SSA). The access permit is issued based on a person's need for access (Article 27 § 1 SSA). The exact procedure is laid down in the Government of the Republic Regulation No. 216.[49] A person applying for an access permit must be an Estonian citizen at least eighteen years old or a legal person in private law registered in Estonia (Article 28 § 2 SSA). The applicant must pass a security

[49] See Government of the Republic Regulation No. 216 on the approval of Procedure for Protection of State Secrets and Procedure for Issue of Permits for Access to State Secrets of 8 July 1999, RT I 1999, 61, 622, an English translation of this regulation can be found at http://www.legaltext.ee/text/en/X40004K4.htm.

check (Article 29 SSA). Grounds on which the access permit can be refused are listed in Article 31 SSA.

Procedural Rules

General principles laid down in Article 4 PIA state that access to information shall be ensured for every person in the fastest and easiest manner possible. Conditions for the applicant are laid down in Article 13 et seq. A request can be made orally or in writing. The application must contain the applicant's name and surname, details of the applicant through which the public authority can release the information, the content of the information requested or the type, name and content of the document requested and the manner in which the request must be complied with. Public authorities are obliged to clearly explain the procedure, to assist applicants in every way, to promptly send the applicant to a competent official if the applicant has addressed the wrong official and to promptly ask for additional information if the request is incomplete (Article 15). A request for information shall be complied with promptly, but not later than within five working days (Article 18 § 1). The term can be extended by fifteen working days (Article 19). The applicant shall be informed about this and the underlying reasons within five working days.

According to Article 23 PIA a public authority *shall* refuse to comply with a request for information if the authority does not possess the requested information, does not know who possesses it, and is unable to identify the holder of the requested information; compliance with the request for information is impossible because the request does not specify what information is needed; the applicant has not paid the relevant state fee or other expenses relating to the request. A public authority *may* refuse a request if the has already been issued the requested information and does not justify the need to obtain the information for a second time; the information requested from a natural person or a legal person in private law does not concern the performance of public duties; compliance would require a change in the organisation of work of the holder of information, hinder the performance of public duties imposed thereon or require unnecessarily disproportionate expenses due to the large volume of requested information; the request for information cannot be complied with by a single release of information; compliance would require the information to be additionally systematised and analysed and new information would have to be documented. The latter requests are deemed to be petitions and are addressed pursuant to the procedure prescribed in the Response to Petitions Act. Access *may* also be denied if the person making the request for information has been divested of active legal capacity by a court or if there is no address or phone number concerning the person making the request for information. When possible, refusal shall be communicated to the applicant within five working days (Article 23 § 3 PIA).

Legal Remedies

According to Article 4 § 5 PIA, every person has the right to contest a restriction on access to information if such restriction violates the individual's rights or freedoms. Article 44 § 2 states that, within the limits of competence, a superior body or agency shall exercise supervision over compliance with the PIA. A person whose rights under the PIA are violated may challenge the relevant decision before this supervisory body or commence a procedure before an administrative court (Article 46).

With regard to state secrets, the SSA does not contain any legal remedies for persons wanting to challenge a negative decision upon their request for an access permit. However, where an administrative court procedure is possible, the SSA amends the Code of Administrative Offences allowing judges by virtue of their office to access state secrets in order to perform duties which have been assigned to them (§ 39 SSA).

Institutional Structure

The Chancellor of Justice is an independent official who reviews legislation of general application of the legislative and the executive powers and of local governments for conformity with the Estonian Constitution. Each year, the Chancellor of Justice presents his findings in a report to the National Parliament. The report contains information on legislation of general application regarding the right to information, Article 44 of the Constitution.

Finland

Legislation on Access to Information

- Article 12 of the New Constitution Act of Finland of 11 June 1999[50]
- Act no. 621/99 on the Openness of Government Activities of 21 May 1999, entered into force on 1 December 1999[51]

Scope

Article 12, Freedom of expression and right of access to information, of the New Constitution Act of Finland reads:

> Everyone has the freedom of expression. Freedom of expression entails the right to express, disseminate and receive information, opinions and other communications without prior prevention by anyone. More detailed provisions on the exercise of the freedom of expression are laid down by an Act. Provisions on restrictions relating to pictorial programs that are necessary for the protection of children may be laid down by an Act. Documents and recordings in the possession of the authorities are public, unless their publication has for compelling reasons been specifically restricted by an Act. Everyone has the right of access to public documents and recordings.

Rules concerning access to documents are laid down in the Act on the Openness of Government Activities (Openness Act). According to Article 5, of the act 'document' is defined as a written or visual presentation, and also as a message relating to a given topic or subject-matter and consisting of signs which, by virtue of the use to which they are put, are meant to be taken as a whole, but are decipherable only by means of a computer, an audio or video recorder or some other technical device. Access is, however, limited to 'official documents', which are defined as documents in the possession of an authority and prepared by an authority or a person in the service of an authority, or documents delivered to an authority for the consideration of a matter or otherwise in connection with a matter within the competence or duties of the authority.

The following documents are not considered as 'official':

> (1) a letter or other document sent to a person in the service of an authority or to an elected official because of another task performed or position held by the recipient;

50 An unofficial English translation of the Finnish Constitution can be found at http://www.finlex.fi/pdf/saadkaan/E9990731.PDF.

51 An English translation of this Act can be found at http://www.om.fi/1184.htm.

(2) notes kept by a person in the service of an authority or a person commissioned by an authority and such drafts which have not yet been released for presentation or other consideration;
(3) documents procured for in-service training, information retrieval or any other comparable internal activity of an authority;
(4) a document given to an authority for the performance of a task on behalf of a private party, or prepared for this purpose;
(5) a document left with or handed in to an authority as lost property.

The Openness Act applies to documents prepared for negotiations or communications between persons in the service of authorities or between authorities and private individuals or corporations acting on their behalf, or for other comparable internal activities of such authorities, only if the documents contain such information that, according to the archives legislation, they are to be archived. However, if the documents are archived, the authority may order that access to them may be granted only by permission of the authority.

According to Article 4 Openness Act, 'authorities' are defined as state administrative authorities and other state agencies and institutions, courts of law and other bodies for the administration of law, state enterprises, municipal authorities, the Bank of Finland, Parliamentary agencies and institutions, but not Parliament.[52] Also considered as authorities are independent boards, consultative bodies, commissions, committees, working groups, investigators, as well as auditors of municipalities and federations of municipalities, and other comparable organs appointed for the performance of a given task on the basis of an Act, a Decree or a decision of some of the aforementioned authorities. The provisions for the authorities also apply to corporations, institutions, foundations and private individuals appointed for the performance of a public task on the basis of an Act, a Decree or a provision or order issued by virtue of an Act or a Decree, when they exercise public authority.

The Openness Act distinguishes between documents that have entered the public domain and those that have not. Access to official documents in the first place relates to access to official documents in the public domain. Article 6 of the Openness Act lists the ways in which a document is supposed to have entered the public domain. Access to documents that have not yet entered the public domain shall be granted at the discretion of the authority (Article 9). Access to secret documents or their contents shall not be granted, unless specified otherwise in the Openness Act. Secrecy obligations are provided for in chapter 6 of the Openness Act and will be discussed below. Articles 11 and 12 deal specifically with access to documents of importance for parties in a judicial procedures and access to personal data.

[52] See O. Mäenpää, *Right of access to documents: new Finnish legislation*, in *Freedom of Information Review*, April 2001, p. 14-21.

Point of Departure

Under the Openness Act, official documents are in the public domain unless specifically provided otherwise by law.

Exceptions

According to Article 22 of the Openness Act, an official document shall be secret if it has been so provided for in the Openness Act or another act, or if it has been declared secret by an authority by virtue of an act, or if it contains information covered by the duty of non-disclosure as provided for in an act. Article 24 contains a list of 32 categories of documents that are, in principle, secret. The interests protected are:

- personal integrity and other important personal interests in health care, social services, taxation or public supervision;
- protection of private business interests;
- the economic interests of the State and the municipalities;
- protection of the environment;
- prevention and prosecution of crime;
- safeguarding judicial proceedings and data protection;
- the security of the state and its relations with foreign powers; and
- national defence.[53]

Some of the 32 categories of secret documents are absolute. However, the majority are subject to one of two harm tests. The first states that access shall be denied if access would injure or compromise the interest invoked. The second test has the opposite presumption: access shall be denied, unless it is obvious that access will not violate or compromise the interest invoked. According to Article 23, authorities are under a duty to not disclose secret documents. However, special circumstances can justify granting access (chapter 7). When only a part of the document is secret, where possible, access shall be granted to the public part of the document (Article 10).

On July 2004, Act no. 588/2004 on International Information Security Obligations (Security Act) entered into force.[54] This act contains provisions on official measures for the fulfilment of international information security obligations. According to section 3 of the Security Act, the provisions of the Openness Act apply, in so far as not provided otherwise in the Security Act. Once information is marked as protected information, it shall be kept secret (section 6 Security Act). An authority processing protected information shall see to it that only persons who need the information for the performance of their task have access to it (section 6 Security Act).

---

53 See Mäenpää (2001), p. 17/8.

54 The English text of this act was provided by the Finnish representative in answer to the questionnaire.

Procedural Rules

A request for an official document must be sufficiently detailed. The applicant must be able to use official diaries and indexes to specify the document. Applicants are not obliged to identify themselves nor do they have to provide reasons for their request, unless provisions in the Openness Act require so (Article 13 Openness Act). Access to a document in the public domain shall be granted as soon as possible, and in any event within two weeks from the date on which the authority received the application (Article 14). Because of practical difficulties, this time limit can be extended to one month. Applications made to the wrong authority may be forwarded to the right authority (Article 15).

Legal Remedies

An authority's decision is subject to appeal to an administrative court, as provided in the Act on Administrative Judicial Procedure (Act no. 586/96).

Institutional Structure

It is common practice in Finland that major law reforms are regularly evaluated. In accordance with this practice, the Openness Act was evaluated in 2003.[55]

Other Characteristics

Chapter 5 of the Openness Act contains provisions on the duty of the authorities to promote access and good practices in information management. According to these provisions, authorities must actively produce and disseminate information on their activities. Good practices in information management deals with the obligation to see to the appropriate availability, usability, protection, integrity and other matters of quality pertaining to documents and information management systems (Article 18). More detailed rules concerning good practices in information management are laid down in decree no. 1030/1999.[56]

Other activities in the field of transparency

In order to enhance public authorities' compliance with the Openness Act, a compilation of guidelines, instructions and recommendations has been put into force.[57] Guidelines on the active promotion of transparency and the encouragement of civil participation have also been issued.[58]

---

55 The Government report can be found in Finnish and in Swedish at the website of the Finnish Parliament http://www.eduskunta.fi.

56 An unofficial translation can be found at http://www.finlex.fi/pdf/saadkaan/E9991030.PDF.

57 These can be found at the website of the Finnish Ministry of Justice http://www.om.fi/333.htm.

58 See the Guidelines for Government Communication to be found on the website of the Prime Minister's Office http://www.government.fi/vn/liston/vnk.lsp?r=1069&k=en&old=1100 and see the Civil Participation Policy Programme at http://www.government.fi/vn/liston/base.lsp?r=40242&k=en.

France

Legislation on Access to Information

- Act no. 78-753 on various measures for improved relations between the civil service and the public on various arrangements of administrative, social and fiscal nature of 17 July 1978 as amended by Act no. 79-587 and Act no. 2000-321[59]
- Act no. 79-18 on the consultation of archives of 3 January 1979 as amended by Act no. 2000-321[60]

Scope

Article 1 of Act no. 78-753 part 1 of the Act specifies and guarantees 'the right of everyone to information as far as the freedom of access to administrative documents is concerned'. The right applies to all administrative documents held by public authorities (Article 2).

'Administrative documents' mean 'any files, reports, studies, records, minutes, statistics, orders, instructions, ministerial circulars, memoranda or replies containing an interpretation of positive law or a description of administrative procedures, recommendations, forecasts and decisions originating from the State, territorial authorities, public institutions or from public or private-law organisations managing a public service' (Article 1). These documents may be written, audio or video recordings, documents on a data-processing medium or documents obtainable through any currently used automated process (Article 1).

Acts of parliamentary bodies, opinions of the *Conseil d'État* and administrative courts, certain documents of the State Audit Office (*Cour des comptes*) and the regional audit chambers and documents regarding the investigation of complaints referred to the national Ombudsman are not considered as 'administrative documents' (Article 1).

Article 2 limits the scope of the right of access to *finalised* documents. Furthermore, preparatory documents relating to an administrative decision fall outside the scope of the right to access prior to the final decision. The right to access cannot be exercised with regard to documents that are already public or documents created in connection with service contracts involving one or more specific persons.

---

59 The consolidated text of Act no. 78-753 with regard to access to administrative documents is translated in English and can be found at http://www.cada.fr/uk/center2.htm. The consolidated text in French is available at http://www.legifrance.gouv.fr/texteconsolide/PPEAV.htm. The French text of Act no. 2000-321 can be found via http://www.legifrance.gouv.fr.

60 The French text can be found via http://www.legifrance.gouv.fr.

Point of Departure

Everyone has access to finalised administrative documents held by public authorities, unless exceptions provided by law apply.

Exceptions

Exceptions are listed in Article 6 Act no. 78-753. The first set of exceptions are mandatory and are subject to a harm test. Access *shall* not be granted when disclosure would be harmful to:

- the secrecy of the deliberations of the Government and the executive authorities;
- national defence secrets;
- the conduct of France's foreign policy;
- State security, public safety or security of individuals;
- the currency and public finance;
- the proper conduct of proceedings begun before jurisdictions or of operations preliminary to such proceedings, unless authorisation is given by the competent authority;
- investigations by the competent authorities to detect tax and customs offences;
- in general, secrets protected by the law

The following documents shall not be disclosed, where:

- disclosure would prejudice the secrecy of personal life and personal files, medical secrets or to business or industrial secrets;
- documents provide an evaluation or value judgement on a natural person, referred to by his/her name or easily identifiable;
- documents describing the behaviour of a person, the disclosure of which could harm the latter.

In these instances access can only be granted to the person concerned.

Procedural Rules

Act no. 78-753 contains no rules on the way in which an application must be made. Article 2 gives authorities the possibility to deny a request for disclosure when requests appear unreasonable, because of the number of documents requested or because of the repetitive or systematic nature of the requests.

Access can be given on the spot, without any cost, unless preservation of the documents prevents this. Access can also be given by handing over a copy at the applicant's expense, provided that the expense does not exceed the reproduction costs (Article 4).

Refusal of access must be notified to the applicant in writing and must state reasons for the refusal (Article 7). Act no. 78-753 does not contain any time limits for the authorities.

Legal Remedies

Applicants can lodge an appeal against a decision of an authority to an administrative court. Before doing so, the applicant is obliged to submit a complaint to the Committee of Access to Administrative Documents (*Commission d'Accès aux Documents Administratifs*, CADA). The CADA can issue recommendations (Article 5 Act no. 78-753).

Institutional Structure

The CADA was created in accordance with Article 5 Act no. 78-753. The CADA oversees compliance with freedom of access to administrative documents and public archives under the conditions of Act no. 78-753 and Act. No. 79-18 on the consultation of archives. The CADA may issue recommendations following the complaint of a person who claims to be the victim of an unjustified refusal of access to an administrative document. Moreover, the CADA may advise competent authorities on any subject related to the implementation of the two acts. The CADA produces an annual report on the way in which effect is given to the rules on access to administrative documents.[61]

[61] The very informative website of the CADA can be found at http://www.cada.fr.

Germany

Legislation on Access to Information

- Article 29 of the Act on administrative procedures (*Verwaltungsverfahrensgesetz*) of 25 May 1976[62]
- For the *Länder*:
  - Berlin: *Berliner Informationsfreiheitsgesetz* (BIFG) of 15 October 1999, GVBl. 1999, 561
  - Brandenburg: *Akteneinsichts- und Informationszugangsgesetz* of 10 March 1998, GVBl. I, 46
  - Nordrhein-Westfalen: *Informationsfreiheitsgesetz Nordrhein-Westfalen* of 27 November 2001, GVBl 2001, 806
  - Schleswig-Holstein: *Informationsfreiheitsgesetz* of 9 February 2000, GVOBl. 166[63]

Scope

At the federal level, no general right of access to documents exists. According to Article 29 of the Act on administrative procedures, only persons involved in an administrative procedure have a right to access documents; this relates strictly to the procedure and to the defence their legal interest. Currently, a Federal Act on Freedom of Information (Federal Information Act) is being discussed. The German Parliament has completed the first reading of this new law on 17 December 2004.[64] Its entry into force is likely in mid-2005.[65] The Act will grant an enforceable right of access to official information permanently held by the federal administration in the exercise of its functions according to public law.

Of the *Länder*, only four have specific rules on freedom of information: Berlin, Brandenburg, Nordrhein-Westfalen and Schleswig-Holstein. States without an act on access to documents justify their inaction by referring to the discussions about the new law at the federal level. This review will restrict itself to the Berliner Freedom of Information Act (*Berliner Informationsfreiheitsgesetz,*

---

62 The German text can be found via http://www.gesetze.2me.net/vwvf/.

63 The German texts of these acts can be found at http://www.hfv-speyer.de/hill/Akteneinsicht.htm#Nationale%20Gesetze.

64 A press release can be found at http://www.datenschutzzentrum.de/material/themen/presse/20041217-ifg.htm.

65 This information is distracted from the German answers to the questionnaire. In the following, all the information on the proposed Federal Information Act is distracted from these answers. An inaccurate proposal of the new Freedom of Information Act (originating from 2000) can be found at: http://www.transparente-verwaltung.de/ifgbund.pdf.

BIFG). This restriction does not imply that no differences exist between the four acts of the *Länder*.[66]

The BIFG grants everyone (*'Jeder'*), i.e. also legal persons,a right to *access to* or *information on* documents that are held by public authorities.[67] Documents mean all written, electronic, optical, acoustic or differently held information and other recordings, in particular papers, magnetic tapes, diskettes, films, photographs, audio tapes, plans, diagrams, images and maps, as long as they serve an official purpose.

Point of Departure

In Germany, the principle of official secrecy has traditionally blocked access to official information.[68] According to this principle all information held by the public administration is secret. At the federal level, access is only possible when a special interest justifies the disclosure of information. On the other hand, in the four *Länder* everyone has the right to access, unless a restriction applies.

In the future, the Federal Information Act will in principle grant access to all documents, unless exceptions apply.

Exceptions

In the BIFG, exceptions are laid down in Articles 5 through 12. A distinction can be drawn between mandatory and discretionary exceptions.

With regard to business information, Article 7 prohibits the disclosure of information if it is confidential business information, or if the disclosure causes damage to the company concerned, unless the interest in disclosure counterbalances the interest of the company. The same test applies to the protection of personal data (Article 6).[69] Disclosure is also forbidden if it would prejudice the proper course of judicial procedures and criminal prosecution (Article 9). Another exception is made for the protection of the decision-making process (Article 10). If a decision is not yet finalised, access to documents which are directly related to the decision cannot be accessed.

Apart from these exceptions, access shall be denied when disclosure of the requested document would cause severe disadvantages to Germany or one of the *Länder* (Article 11). However, if denial of access only pertains to certain parts of a document or file, the rest of the document can in principle be made available (Article 12).

---

[66] See for an extensive comparison and for other information about the German access rules S. Frenzel, Zugang zu Informationen der deutschen Behörden. Mit einder Dokumentation aus- und inländische Rechtsquellen, 2000, found at http://www.hfv-speyer.de/publ/frenzel131.pdf.

[67] This refers to courts and the Public Attorney's Office only insofar as they deal with administrative tasks.

[68] See the German results of the Council of Europe questionnaire, p. 78.

[69] As regards personal data, disclosure is also prohibited if access to documents is mainly pursued for private interests.

The future Federal Information Act creates exceptions for the protection of public interests (if a negative impact can be proven by the administrative authority), decision-making (if the aim of the decision would be defeated), personal data (requires a balance of interest) and trade secrets (requires consent by the affected person). Access to classified information or information held by the security and intelligence agencies shall be denied.

Procedural Rules

Article 13 BIFG contains rules concerning the form and the substance of a request for access to documents. A request can be made in writing or orally. The document requested must be described and the application must be sent to the competent authority. If a wrong authority is addressed, that authority is obliged to send the application immediately to the right authority.

The publication, storage or collection of the received information for commercial purposes is prohibited (Article 13 § 7).

While a request for access to documents must be dealt with immediately, it must be preceded by an examination of admissibility (Article 14 § 1). Where a request is admissible and the rights of third parties are not involved, access can be granted upon an oral or written request. Following a justified oral request, access must be granted or information on the substance must be given immediately. Following a justified written request, the applicant will receive a decision with information on how to obtain access.

A refusal to grant access must be communicated in writing, within two weeks. In its reasoning, the public authority must inform the applicant about the content of the withheld documents, insofar as this does not lead to the disclosure of confidential information. If the initial request was oral, the refusal must also be in writing if the applicant so requested (Article 15 § 1).

Legal Remedies

If an application is rejected, the applicant can lodge an administrative appeal to the administrative authority superior to the one which refused the access. If the decision was made by the highest regional administrative authority, appeal to an administrative court is possible (Article 14 § 3 BIFG).

Institutional Structure

According to Article 18 BIFG and the other three acts on freedom of information of Brandenburg, Nordrhein-Westfalen and Schleswig-Holstein, Commissioners for Data Protection and Access to Information are appointed. Everyone has the right to contact these Commissioners. The Commissioner can give (non-binding) recommendations.[70]

---

[70] See the German results of the Council of Europe questionnaire, p. 81.

Greece

Legislation on Access to Information

- Article 5A and 10 of the Greek Constitution of 1975[71]
- Article 5 of Act no. 2690/1999, the Administrative Procedure Code, of 9 March 1999[72]
- Article 16 of Act no. 1599/1986 on the Relations between citizens and the state and other provisions[73]

Scope

Article 5A § 1 of the Greek Constitution reads:

> All persons are entitled to information, as specified by law. Restrictions to this right may be imposed by law only insofar as they are absolutely necessary and justified for reasons of national security, of combating crime or of protecting rights and interests of third parties.

Article 10 § 3 adds:

> The competent service or authority is obliged to reply to requests for information and for issuing documents, especially certificates, supporting documents and attestations within a set deadline not exceeding 60 days, as specified by law. In case this deadline elapses without action or in case of unlawful refusal, in addition to any other sanctions and consequences at law, special compensation is also paid to the applicant, as specified by law.

Rules on access to documents are further specified in Article 5 of Act 2690/1999. According to § 1 of this article *any interested party* is entitled, by written application, to be informed of administrative documents. The official report of 9 June 1999 of the Committee that prepared the draft Code explicitly states that every natural or legal person enjoys the right of access to administrative documents, without any legal interest having to be proven.[74] However, preceding case law of the Greek Council of State based on Act 1599/1986 (see below), suggests that the Council will require something like a 'justified interest'.[75]

---

71 An English translation can be found at http://confinder.richmond.edu/greek_2001.html.

72 An English translation can be found at http://unpan1.un.org/intradoc/groups/public/documents/UNTC/UNPAN001820.pdf.

73 A German translation can be found at http://www.uni-frankfurt.de/~sobotta/greece.htm. General information about this law is distracted from the Report of the European Commission of 9 October 2000, p. 9-11.

74 See Report of the European Commission of 9 October 2000, p. 10.

75 *Ibid.*

'Administrative documents' are documents *drawn up* by public authorities, such as reports, studies, minutes, statistical data, circulars, replies of the Administration, opinions and resolutions. Article 1 of Act 2690/1999 declares the Act applicable to the State, local communities and other legal entities under public law. Access to documents *drawn up* by private legal entities that belong to the public sector is subject to the rules of Article 16 of Act 1599/1986, which was – until the entry into force of Act 2690/1999 – the only Act containing rules on access to documents and which was until then applicable to public authorities as well. In Act 2690/1999, administrative documents are discerned from private documents. However, a clear definition of private documents is not given. According to Article 5 § 2 any person having a special legal interest is entitled, by written application, to be informed of private documents *held* by public authorities. The documents must be related to a case pending before or handled by the public authority.

Point of Departure

Act 2690/1999 allows every interested person access to administrative documents, unless exceptions under Act 2690/1999 apply. Persons with a special legal interest are entitled to have access to private documents, unless exceptions under Act 2690/1999 apply.

Exceptions

Exceptions can be found in § 3 of Article 5 Act 2690/1999. Firstly, absolute exceptions are cases where the document concerns the private or family life of a third party or where there is a violation of confidentiality created by special provisions. The right to access *is not applicable* in these cases. Secondly, where documents refer to discussions of the Council of Ministers, competent authorities *may* refuse access. The latter is a discretionary exception, requiring the competent authority to balance the interests involved. Lastly, if the disclosure would *substantially obstruct* the investigation of judicial, police, military or administrative authorities regarding criminal or administrative offences, access *may* be refused. This exception requires a harm test and a balance of interests.

Procedural Rules

Right to access is exercised by studying the document on the spot or by issuing a copy, unless reproduction prejudices the original (Article 5 § 4 Act 2690/1999).

Refusal of a request for access shall be sent to the applicant in writing within one month after the submission of the application (Article 5 § 6 Act 2690/1999).

Legal Remedies

General rules on judicial protection apply.[76] Firstly, administrative appeal to the same authority that refused access is possible, but an appeal can also be lodge to an authority hierarchically superior to the refusing authority. Finally, judicial appeal to an administrative court is possible.

According to Article 10 § 3 of the Greek Constitution, a person may claim special compensation in cases of unlawful refusal or expiry of the time limit.

Other Characteristics

Article 5 § 2 of the Greek Constitution reads:

> All persons are entitled to participate in the Information Society. Facilitation of access to electronically handled information, as well as of the production, exchange and diffusion thereof constitutes an obligation of the State, always in observance of the guarantees of Articles 9, 9A and 19.

Articles 9, 9A and 19 of the Greek Constitution provide rules concerning the protection of a person's home, private and family life (9), personal data (9A) and the secrecy of correspondence (19).

76 The following information is taken from Prakke & Kortmann (2004), p. 412/3.

Hungary

Legislation on Access to Information

- Article 61 of the Hungarian Constitution[77]
- Act LXIII on the Protection of Personal Data and the Disclosure of Data of Public Interest of 27 October 1992[78]
- Act LXV on State Secrets and Official Secrets of 31 December 1995[79]

Scope

Article 61 § 1 of the Hungarian Constitution reads:

> In the Republic of Hungary, everyone has the right to the free declaration of his views and opinions, and has the right of access to information of public interest, and also the freedom to disseminate such information.

In Hungary, protection of personal data and freedom of information are jointly regulated in Act LXIII on the Protection of Personal Data and the Disclosure of Data of Public Interest (Act LXIII). Article 2 § 4 defines 'data of public interest' as any data (information), not falling under the definition of personal data, processed by an organ or person performing a state or local government function or other public function determined by a rule of law, or any information pertaining to the activities thereof. Specified rules on public access to information of public interest can be found in chapter III of this Act.

Point of Departure

Everyone has the right to access to information of public interest, unless legally defined exceptions apply.

Exceptions

General rules on exceptions are found in Article 19 § 3 Act LXIII. Information classified as 'state' or 'official secrets' are exempted from the right to access. These state and official secrets are regulated by Act LXV on State Secrets and Official Secrets (Act LXV). Another exception is made for data that is classified on grounds of an obligation resulting from an international agreement. By order of law, other restrictions may apply to protect interests of:

---

77 An English translation can be found at http://www.lectlaw.com/files/into5.htm. See for an extensive overview of the freedom of expression and access to information http://www.helsinki.hu/docs/expression010607.pdf.

78 An English translation can be found at http://abiweb.obh.hu/dpc/legislation/1992_LXIIIa.htm.

79 An English translation can be found at http://faculty.maxwell.syr.edu/asroberts/foi/library/hungary_secrecy_95.pdf.

a) national defence;
b) national security;
c) criminal investigation and crime prevention;
d) financial or foreign exchange policy of the State;
e) international relations and relations to international organisations;
f) judicial proceedings.

Information prepared in connection with decision-making will not be made public within twenty years of its creation (Article 19 § 5 Act LXIII). However, upon request the head of the authority may grant access to this information.

Act LXV distinguishes between a *state secret* and an *official secret*. Information considered a 'state secret' is information contained in a list of 149 categories (attached to Act LXV) *and* where the classifying authority has determined that disclosure would *without doubt damage or jeopardise* the interests of the Republic of Hungary related to defence, national security, criminal investigation and criminal prevention, central finance and exchange policy, foreign affairs, international relations and judicature (Chapter II subsection 1, section 3 Act LXV). The length of secrecy of state secrets may not exceed ninety years. 'Office secrets' are so classified by competent authorities if they *would damage* the orderly operation of an organisation fulfilling a state or public duty, and *would prevent* it from completing its scope of tasks and exercising its competence (Chapter II, subsection 1, section 4 Act LXV). Official secrets may be kept secret for a maximum of twenty years. Unclassified information will not be considered a state or official secret, even when the information meets the requirements of Act LXV.[80]

Access to classified information can be granted by an examination or accessibility permit which can be given to a person with a special interest, e.g. the information contains personal data or access is needed for the purpose of performing a state or public duty (Chapter IV, subsection 2 Act LXV). If the law does not provide otherwise, a concerned person may access data classified as an official secret without restriction (Chapter IV, subsection 3 Act LXV). However, authorised persons are under a 'secret keeping obligation'; they are not allowed to transfer the information to unauthorised persons (Chapter V, subsection 1, section 16 Act LXV).

Procedural Rules

An application to access information of public interest must be completed as soon as possible, at the latest within fifteen days (Article 20 § 1 Act LXIII). If the

80 See on this topic and for a general analysis of freedom of information in Hungary László Majtényi, *Freedom of Information in Hungary*, to be found at http://unpan1.un.org/intradoc/groups/public/documents/nispacee/unpan006566.pdf, pp. 145-150.

application is rejected, the applicant has to be notified in writing within eight days (Article 20 § 2 Act LXIII). Actual costs may be charged.

Legal Remedies

If an application is refused, within thirty days an applicant may institute court proceedings (Article 21 § 1 Act LXIII). The burden of proof lies with the authority. If the applicant's claim is granted, the court shall order the authority to disclose the requested information (Article 21 § 7 Act LXIII). Legal remedy rules under Act LXIII also apply to the rejection of an application for access to state secrets and official secrets (Chapter IV, subsection 1, section 15, subsection 3 and 4 Act LXV).

Applicants can also complain to the Data Protection Commissioner (Article 27 Act LXIII).

Section 177/B of Act IV on the Criminal Code of 1978 states that any person who in violation of the statutory provisions governing access to public information, fails to comply with the obligation to provide any public information, falsifies or renders inaccessible any public information or conveys or publishes any public information that is untrue or has been falsified, is guilty of a misdemeanour punishable by up to two years imprisonment, community service or a fine.[81] These penalties shall be upgraded if they are committed for unlawful financial gain or advantage.

Institutional Structure

According to Article 23 Act LXIII, the Parliament shall elect a Data Protection Commissioner (DPC).[82] The DPC shall

a) supervise compliance with this Act and other rules of law on data processing;
b) investigate complaints lodged with him;
c) ensure the maintenance of the data protection register;
d) promote a uniform application of statutory provisions on the processing of personal data and on public access to data of public interest; and
e) exercise the powers and perform the tasks as laid down in this Act.[83]

The DPC has the power to call on the competent authority to change or annul a contested decision if it determines that refusal of access was unjustified (Article 26 § 4 Act LXIII). Within thirty days, the competent authority may challenge the DPC's decision before the Metropolitan Court of Justice.

---

81 An English translation of these sections of the Criminal Code can be found at http://abiweb.obh.hu/dpc/legislation/1978_IV_177a.htm.

82 The website of the Data Protection Commissioner can be found at http://abiweb.obh.hu/dpc/index.htm.

83 Article 24 Act LXIII.

The authorities shall annually report to the DPC on refused applications and the reasons for their refusal (Article 20 Act LXIII).

Other Characteristics

Act LXIII contains a few provisions on the active promotion of open government. Article 19 § 1 requires that authorities promote and ensure accurate and prompt information for the general public concerning matters within their sphere of competence. Under § 2, these authorities shall regularly publish or otherwise enable access to the most important information about their activities.

Other Activities in the Field of Transparency

In 2002, the Ministry of Informatics and Communication was created. The Ministry's central mission is to find solutions to the new challenges of the information age as well as to aid and facilitate the emergence of the knowledge economy and knowledge society.[84] In order to reach this objective, the Ministry has identified five strategic goals, this includes requiring that all public information be available online, providing equal access to information for all citizens and protecting personal, human, social and community rights. The Ministry maintains a homepage devoted to ongoing deliberations on the electronic freedom of information Act.[85]

84 See the website of the Ministry of Informatics and Communication at http://en.ihm.gov.hu/.

85 To be found in Hungarian at http://www.ihm.gov.hu/infoszabadsag/konferencia.

Ireland

Legislation on Access to Information

- Freedom of Information Act, Act no. 13 of 21 April 1997[86]
- Freedom of Information (Amendment) Bill of 9 April 2003[87]
- Official Secrets Act, 1963[88]

Scope

The Freedom of Information Act (FOIA) contains rules for access to information in the possession of public bodies in general and for access to personal information in particular.[89] The FOIA entered into force on 21 April 1997. Nearly five years later, the FOIA was substantially amended by the FOIA (Amendment) Bill. One of the main reasons for this amendment was the fact that Cabinet Documents would be available after five years.[90] With the amendment this period was extended to ten years. Below, the FOIA including its amendments will be described.[91]

According to the sub-title the FOIA

> enable[s] members of the public to obtain access, to the greatest extent possible consistent with THE PUBLIC INTEREST AND THE RIGHT TO PRIVACY, TO INFORMATION IN THE POSSESSION OF PUBLIC BODIES

Section 6 § 1 FOIA confers a right to every person to access to any record held by a public body. By 'record' is meant:

> any memorandum, book, plan, map, drawing, diagram, pictorial or graphic work or other document, any photograph, film or recording (whether of sound or images or both), any form in which data (within the meaning of the Data Protection Act, 1988) are held, any other form (including machine-readable form) or thing in which information is held or stored manually, mechanically or electronically and anything that is a part or a copy, in any form, of any of the foregoing or is

---

86 To be found at http://www.oic.gov.ie/2132/FREEACT.PDF.

87 To be found at http://www.oireachtas.ie/documents/bills28/acts/2003/a903.pdf.

88 To be found at http://www.irishstatutebook.ie/1963_1.html.

89 A separate act on data protection exists since 1988. This Data Protection Act also contains rules on access to personal information. Both acts can be invoked by individuals. The Data Protection Act (including the amendment of 2003) can be found via http://www.dataprotection.ie/docs/Home/4.htm.

90 See M. McDonagh, *The Honeymoon is over: Ireland rows back on FoI*, in *Freedom of Information Review*, October 2003, p. 78-84.

91 See for a comparison between the old and the new text McDonagh, *ibid.*, and M. McDonagh, *Freedom of Information in Ireland: Five Years On*, posted on 22 September 2003 on freedominfo.org, to be found at http://www.freedominfo.org/reports/ireland/ireland.pdf.

a combination of two or more of the foregoing and a copy, in any form, of a record shall be deemed, for the purposes of this Act, to have been created at the same time as the record.[92]

The FOIA provides a list of what constitutes a 'public body'. The list consists of 67 central governmental agencies. However, the FOIA foresaw additions to this list and in December 2003 the number of bodies was approaching 400.[93]

Section 46 FOIA lists seven categories of records that are excluded from the scope of the FOIA. Excluded are, e.g., records held by the courts, records relating to the President and records whose disclosure would lead to the revelation of the identity of a person who has provided information to a public body in relation to the enforcement of criminal law.

The scope of the FOIA is also limited in time. Documents created before April 1998 are not covered by the FOIA, unless they contain personal information or are necessary to understand documents created after April 1998.[94]

Point of Departure

Subject to the provisions of the FOIA, every person has access to any record held by a public body.

Exceptions

First of all, access to records can be refused on administrative grounds. If an individual does not comply with the requirements listed in section 7, access may be refused (section 10 FOIA). The requirements are explained below under 'Procedural rules'.

The FOIA contains a variety of exceptions, not only with regard to protected interests, but also concerning harm and public interest tests. The exceptions are set out in Part III of the FOIA. Twelve grounds for exemption can be distinguished; these include:[95]

1 meetings of government (section 19)
2 deliberations of public bodies (section 20)
3 functions and negotiations of public bodies (section 21)
4 parliamentary, court and legal professional privilege (section 22)
5 law enforcement and public safety (section 23)
6 security, defence and international relations (section 24)
7 information obtained in confidence (section 26)

92 Section 2 § 1 FOIA.

93 See the Sixth Report by the Minister for Finance on Freedom of Information, January – December 2003, to be found at http://www.foi.gov.ie, p. 7.

94 Section 6, subsections 4 and 5 FOIA.

95 See also McDonagh (September 2003), p. 8.

8 commercially sensitive information (section 27)
9 personal information (section 28)
10 research and natural resources (section 30)
11 financial and economic interests of the State and public bodies (section 31)
12 enactments relating to non-disclosure of records (section 32).

Some of the exceptions are formulated in mandatory terms, access *shall be refused*: see exceptions 1, 4, 6 (partly), 7, 8 and 9. The mandatory character of exception 9 depends on the substance of the special act concerned. The Official Secrets Act (OSA) – for example – forbids persons to communicate any official (secret) information, unless he or she is duly authorised to do so (Article 4 § 1 OSA). The other exceptions are formulated in discretionary terms.

Subsequently, some of the exceptions are subject to a harm test. This test is formulated in different terms. Access shall or may be refused if disclosure *could reasonably be expected* to 'prejudice' (3, 5) or to 'impair' (5), to have 'a significant, adverse effect' (3), to 'affect adversely' (6), to have 'a serious adverse effect (11) or if disclosure *would be likely* to 'prejudice' (7), to expose ... to serious disadvantage' (10). With regard to certain exceptions, public bodies shall grant access when the *public interest* would, on balance, be better served by granting than by refusing access. See the exceptions 3, 5 (partly), 7, 8, 9, 10 and 11. Access to records containing matters relating to deliberations of public bodies – exception 2 – may be refused if the disclosure would be contrary to public interest. Lastly, some exceptions require consultation with a third party before access can be granted (1, 7, 8 and 9).

With regard to exceptions 5 and 6, a Minister can issue a certificate declaring that a record is exempted from the rules on access. With a certificate, the record cannot be subject to internal review or review by the Information Commissioner (see below). However, an appeal on points of law to the High Court is possible (section 42 § 2 sub a FOIA). Appeal against certificates issued by heads of a Government Department under exception 2, deliberations of public bodies, is not possible.[96]

Procedural Rules

According to Article 7 FOIA, a person who wishes to exercise the right to access shall make a request in writing addressed to the head of the public body concerned stating that the request is made pursuant to the FOIA (§ 1 sub a). The request must contain sufficient particulars in relation to the information concerned so as to enable the record to be identified through reasonable steps (§ 1 sub b), and must specify the form or manner of access (§ 1 sub c). If a person does not fulfil these requirements, access may be refused (section 10 § 1). In order to combat abuse of the access rules, the FOIA provides, since the entering

[96] This possibility was introduced by amendment 2003, see on this McDonagh (September 2003), p. 12.

into force of amendment 2003, for an application fee (section 47).[97] A public body has ten working days to acknowledge receipt of a request (section 7 § 2) and must answer a request within twenty working days (section 8 § 1). Partial access must be granted, if it is practicable to do so (section 13).

Legal Remedies

Where an application is refused, the applicant can generally appeal to the public body to re-examine the case internally. Someone more senior than the person who assessed the original request must review the appeal. This internal review must be completed within fifteen working days (section 14 FOIA). After a second refusal, the applicant may appeal to the independent Office of Information Commissioner (section 34 FOIA). Commissioner decisions are subject to appeal to the High Court and ultimately to the Supreme Court on points of law (section 42).

Institutional Structure

Part IV of the FOIA contains rules on the Information Commissioner.[98] Upon request, the Commissioner can review decisions of public bodies and affirm or annul a decision (section 34). Decisions of the Commissioner are binding for the public body concerned. In order to fulfil its duties, the Commissioner has, e.g., the power to enter premises occupied by a public body (section 37). The Commissioner shall foster and encourage the publication by public bodies of information of relevance to the general public (section 37). Each year the Commissioner shall prepare a report in relation to its activities (section 40). These reports include detailed statistics.[99]

Inside the government, the FOI Central Policy Unit in the Department of Finance oversees application of the act.[100] The Minister of State at the Department of Finance also publishes an annual report.[101]

97 See McDonagh (September 2003), p. 6.

98 The website of the Office of Information Commissioner can be found at http://www.oic.gov.ie/.

99 The reports can be found at the website of the Office of Information Commissioner.

100 See http://www.finance.gov.ie/viewdoc.asp?fn=/documents/foi/cpuindex.htm.

101 The annual reports can be found at http://www.foi.gov.ie.

Italy

Legislation on Access to Information

- Chapter V (on access to administrative documents) of Act no. 241 which establishes new norms in the administrative procedure and right of access to administrative documents of 7 August 1990[102]
- Decree no. 352 of the President of the Republic of 27 June 1992[103]
- Act no. 801, establishment and regulations of the intelligence and security services and discipline of State secrecy, of 24 October 1977[104]

Scope[105]

The Italian Constitution does not provide a legal basis for the right to access to documents or information. The legal basis of this right is Act no. 241 on access to administrative documents (Act 241). Article 22 § 1 of this Act reads:

> To provide for transparency in administrative activity and encourage impartiality in its performance, any person who has an interest to safeguard in legally relevant situations shall have the right of access to administrative documents according to the procedures laid down by the present law.

Thus, only persons with an interest have a right to access to administrative documents. Article 2 § 1 of Decree no. 352 (Decree 352), which specifies procedural rules by implementing Article 24 § 2 Act 241, speaks of any person who has a *personal concrete* interest to safeguard in legally relevant situations.

An administrative document is considered to be any graphic, photographic, cinematic, electromagnetic or other representation of the contents of acts, including internal acts, produced by public administrations or used for purposes of administrative activity (Article 22 § 2).

The right of access applies to the administrative bodies of the state, including special and autonomous bodies, public entities and the providers of public services, as well as guarantee and supervisory authorities (Article 23).

---

[102] An English translation can be found at http://www.governo.it/Presidenza/DICA/documentazione_accesso/normativa/legge241_1990_eng.html.

[103] An English translation can be found at http://www.governo.it/Presidenza/DICA/documentazione_accesso/normativa/dpr352_1992_eng.html.

[104] An English translation can be found at http://www.fas.org/irp/world/italy/intellaw.html.

[105] Rules on access to administrative documents for public participation in local administration are laid down in Act no. 142 governing autonomous local administrations of 8 June 1990, an Italian text of this act can be found via http://www.governo.it/Presidenza/DICA/documentazione_accesso/normativa.html.

Access *is* denied with regard to documents falling within the scope of Article 12 of Act 801 of 24 October 1977 dealing with State secrecy (Article 24 § 1 Act 241).[106] This article reads:

> The documents, proceedings, information, activities, and any matter whose disclosure is apt to jeopardise the integrity of the democratic State, also in relation with international agreements, the defence of the constitutional order, the free exercise of the functions of the constitutional bodies, the independence of the State vis-à-vis other States and its relations with them, the military preparations and defence of the State, are covered by State secrecy.

Point of Departure of the legislation

Any person with an interest to safeguard in legally relevant situations has a right to access administrative documents, unless exceptions based on Act 241 apply.

Exceptions

By issuing decrees, the government can regulate the refusal of access in order to safeguard:

a) security, national defence and international relations;
b) monetary and foreign exchange policy;
c) public order, prevention and repression of crime;
d) the privacy of third parties, persons, groups and enterprises, assuring among other things that the persons affected can inspect the acts involving administrative proceedings knowledge of which is necessary to advance or defend their legal interests.[107]

Also, individual administrative authorities are required to identify, in one or more rules to be issued, the categories of documents produced by them or in any case in their possession that shall be precluded from access owing to the needs set forth above (Article 24 § 4 Act 241).

According to Article 8 § 2 Decree 352, access to documents cannot be denied save when they may do *concrete damage* to the interests mentioned in Act 241. Administrative bodies shall *postpone* access when secrecy is necessary to ensure temporary protection of interests (Article 7 § 2 Decree 352). They are also entitled to postpone access if disclosure can prevent or impede the performance of administrative action (Article 24 § 6 Act 241).

---

[106] An English translation can be found at http://www.fas.org/irp/world/italy/intellaw.html.

[107] Article 24 § 2 Act 241.

Procedural Rules

Requests for access must be motivated and addressed to the administrative body that produced or holds the document (Article 25 § 2 Act 241). Administrative bodies have to answer within thirty days. If no response is given within this period, access is considered to be refused (Article 25 § 4). The person responsible for the access procedure shall give reasons for the refusal. Specific reference must be made to the invoked interest and to the circumstances leading to the refusal (Article 7 § 1 Decree 352).

Legal Remedies

Within thirty days, an appeal against a negative decision is possible to the regional administrative court. The decision of the latter is subject to appeal – again within thirty days – to the Council of State (Article 25 § 5 Act 241).

Institutional Structure

Following Article 27 Act 241, a Committee on Access to Administrative Documents was instituted under the Office of the Prime Minister.[108] According to Article 27 § 5 Act 241:

The Committee shall take care that the principle of full public knowledge of the activity of the public administration is put into practice, in observance of the limitations set forth in the present law; it shall draft an annual report on the transparency of the activity of the public administration, which it shall communicate to the Houses of Parliament and to the Prime Minister; it shall propose to the Government amendments to legislative and regulatory texts useful to achieve the broadest possible guarantee of the right of access referred to in Article 22.

All administrative bodies are required to transmit to the Committee, by a deadline set by the Committee, information and documents that it requests, with the exception of those subject to State secrecy (Article 27 § 6 Act 241).

Other Activities in the Field of Transparency

The Ministry for Innovation and Technology has the task of steering, coordinating and encouraging action by (other) branches of the central administration with a view to defining specific projects, action plans and programs for the deployment of information technologies so as to bring better, more effective and efficient services to citizens and business and, generally, to enhance the economic, social and cultural conditions of the country.[109] The Ministry provides

[108] The website of the Committee on Access to Administrative Documents can be found at http://www.governo.it/Presidenza/ACCESSO/index.html.

[109] The website of the Ministry for Innovation and Technology can be found at http://www.innovazione.gov.it/eng/index.shtml.

guidelines on the transparency of administrative action and on the management of document flows.

Latvia

Legislation on Access to Information

- Freedom of Information Law, adopted on 29 October 1998[110]
- State Secrets Act of 29 October 1996[111]

Scope

The Constitution of Latvia does not contain a specific provision on access to information. However, Article 104 states in general terms that 'everyone has the right to address submissions to State or local government institutions and to receive a materially responsive reply'.[112] Rules on freedom of information are found in the Freedom of Information Law (FOIL) of 1998. Section 2 § 1 of the FOIL specifies 'a uniform procedure by which natural and legal persons are entitled to obtain information from State administrative institutions and Local Government institutions, and to utilise it'.

'Information' is defined as information or compilations of information, in any technically possible format, that is stored or transferred (section 1 § 1 FOIL). Access includes information that is *under the control of* state administrative institutions and local government institutions for the performance of their functions as proscribed by regulation (section 2 § 1). The FOIL does not apply to information exchanged between institutions (section 2 § 4).

The FOIL draws a distinction between generally accessible information and restricted access information (section 3). According to section 4, 'generally accessible information' is any information not categorised as restricted access information. The latter is described below, under 'Exceptions'. Generally accessible information shall be provided to anyone requesting for it. An applicant is not required to give reasons for a request. If information contains partly restricted access information, access to the portion containing generally accessible information is provided (section 10 § 3). If a person wants access to restricted access information, reasons for the request and the purpose for which the information will be used must be stated (section 11 § 4).

Point of Departure

Information shall be accessible to the public in all cases, unless the FOIL specifies otherwise (section 2 § 3 FOIL).

110 An English translation can be found at http://www.ttc.lv/New/lv/tulkojumi/E0029.doc.

111 An unofficial English translation can be found at http://faculty.maxwell.syr.edu/asroberts/foi/library/Latvia_secrecy_trans.pdf.

112 An English translation of the Latvian Constitution can be found at http://www.oefre.unibe.ch/law/icl/lg00000_.html.

Exceptions

Restricted access information is information that can only be used by a restricted group of persons as regards their work or official duties and the disclosure of which hinders or may hinder the activities of the institution concerned, or causes or may cause harm to the lawful interests of persons (section 5 § 1 FOIL). According to section 5 § 2, restricted access information shall be considered information:

1) which has been granted such status by law;
2) which is intended and specified for internal use by an institution;
3) which concerns trade secrets;
4) which concerns the private life of natural persons; or
5) which is related to certifications, examinations, submitted projects, invitations to tender and other assessment processes of a similar nature.

The creator of a document or the head of an institution may classify information as restricted (section 5 § 3).

The first exception refers to the State Secrets Act of 1996. This act regulates the protection of State secrets. Information, the disclosure of which would jeopardise national security or economic or political interests, is considered a state secret and can be qualified as 'Very Secret', 'Secret' or 'Confidential' (section 2 and 3 State Secrets Act). The Cabinet of Ministers determines these classifications (section 4 State Secrets Act). Only Latvian citizens with special permission (a security clearance) can access secret documents (section 9 State Secrets Act).

Other restrictions listed in section 5 § 2 FOIL, except for the last one, are further addressed in sections 6 through 8. Information for internal use is information that an institution requires for the preparation of decisions (section 6). This includes information prepared by advisors or experts, or documents originating from other institutions. Information qualifies as a trade secret, where disclosure would adversely affect the 'ability to compete' of the person who submitted the information (section 7). The Personal Data Protection Law of 2000 protects information regarding the private life of natural persons.[113]

Procedural Rules

Section 11 FOIL lists the requirements of an application. Information may be requested in writing or orally. A written request must contain the applicant's name and surname, domicile or place of residence in Latvia and signature. The request must be formulated as precisely as possible. If a request concerns restricted access information, the applicant has to provide grounds for the request and must specify the purpose for which the information will be used.

[113] An English translation can be found at http://www.dvi.gov.lv/eng/legislation/pdp/.

Access may be refused if the applicant does not fulfil these requirements. Correspondence between the applicant and the institution is considered restricted access information.

Detailed rules on the way information is disclosed can be found in Regulation no. 275 of the Cabinet of Ministers of 3 August 1999.[114] This regulation is based on section 10 § 2 FOIL.

When an institution refuses a written application, it must specify the grounds on which the request was refused and where and within what time period this refusal may be appealed (section 2 § 1 FOIL). If the institution does not possess the requested information, it must tell the applicant which institution has the information (section 2 § 2). Time limits are further specified in the law on Procedures for Reviewing Submissions, Complaints and Proposals in State and Local Government Institutions of 27 October 1994. An institution must answer a request within seven or thirty days, depending on whether the application requires additional information or verification.[115]

Legal Remedies

An applicant has the right to submit a complaint against a refusal to provide information either with the manager of the institution or with a superior institution (section 15 § 1 FOIL). An appeal to a court is possible for any natural or legal person where an institution has infringed the right to obtain information, and the institution:

1) has not provided an answer to the applicant within the time period proscribed by law;
2) has refused to provide information by taking a decision, without legal basis, to grant it the status of restricted access information; or
3) after receiving a written application, has refused to expunge or correct false, incomplete or illegally acquired information regarding a person.[116]

Institutional Structure

The Latvian National Human Rights Office prepares annual reports on the general human rights situation in Latvia. These reports also analyse transparency and questions concerning public access to documents.[117]

---

114 A Latvian text of this regulation can be found at http://www.izm.gov.lv/default.aspx?tabID=3&id=759.

115 See the Latvian results of the Council of Europe questionnaire, p. 102.

116 Section 15 § 2 FOIL.

117 These reports can be found in Latvian at http://www.vcb.lv/zinojumi/.

Other Characteristics

Each institution is obliged to register information, specifying its class, designation, source and for documents, prerequisites to conform with specified law (section 9 § 1 FOIL). Applicants may review the register of generally accessible information (section 9 § 2).

Other Activities in the Field of Transparency

Research on how freedom of information works in practice is carried out by NGOs, for instance, 'Delna', the Latvian branch of *Transparency International.*[118]

[118] See http://www.delna.lv/eng/?sec=94.

Lithuania

Legislation on Access to Information

- Article 25 Lithuanian Constitution of 25 October 1992[119]
- Article 6 Law no. I-1418 on Provision of Information to the Public of 2 July 1996[120]
- Law no. VIII-1524 on the Right to Receive Information from State and Local Authorities of 11 January 2000[121]
- Law no. VIII-1443 on State Secrets and Official Secrets of 25 November 1999[122]

Scope

According to Article 25 § 5 of the Lithuanian Constitution, citizens have the right to obtain all available information *which concerns them* from State agencies in a manner established by law. In Article 6 of the law on Provision of Information to the Public (PIP), every person is granted:

> the right to receive from state and municipal institutions and agencies as well as other budgetary institutions public information relating to their activities, their official documents (copies) as well as information held by the aforementioned institutions about the requesting person.

This right is granted to everyone, including non-citizens. State and municipal institutions and agencies must, according to the procedure under the Law on the Right to Receive Information from State and Municipal Institutions (Information Law) and other laws, provide both public and private information, except where laws specify that private information is not to be disclosed (Article 6 § 3 PIP). According to Article 6 § 7 PIP, institutions and enterprises as well as political parties, trade unions, political and public organisations, and other organisations shall provide creators of public information and other persons, with information relating to their activities in accordance with the procedures established in their articles of association (regulations). The Information Law draws a distinction between information and official documents. This distinction only has consequences for the way in which applications must be made. Requests for access to information can be made orally or in writing, were applications for

---

119 An English translation of the Constitution can be found at http://www.vescc.com/constitution/lithuania-constitution-eng.html.

120 An English translation of this law can be found at http://www.rtk.lt/downloads/PIP_20040501.doc.

121 A Lithuanian text of this law can be found at http://www3.lrs.lt/cgi-bin/preps2?Condition1=102572&Condition2=.

122 An English translation of this law can be found at http://www3.lrs.lt/cgi-bin/preps2?Condition1=128107&Condition2=.

access to official documents must be made in writing (Article 6 Information Law).

Point of Departure

Everyone has the right to access public and private information, unless exceptions apply.

Exceptions

A request for information shall be refused if the information is a state, official, trade or bank secret. Information protected by law, the disclosure of which would damage state security and defence, foreign policy interests and criminal prosecution is also exempted. Information endangering the territorial integrity of the state or that puts public order at risk can be withheld. However, information must be released if non-disclosure would result in serious violations of the law or cause harm to human health (Article 13 § 1 Information Law). In all cases, the institution must verify whether the non-disclosure is necessary in a democratic society and whether the right of the applicant does not outweigh the protection of the interests mentioned above (Article 13 § 2).

Rules on state and official secrets are further addressed in the Law on State Secrets and Official Secrets (State Secrets Law). Article 3 divides classified information into Top Secret, Secret, Confidential and Restricted information. This classification is based on possible damage to the State, its institutions or individuals, and the degree to which such information must be protected. Article 5 State Secrets Law lists categories of classified information. Only Lithuanian citizens that have been granted a special national personnel security clearance certificate can access state and official secrets (Article 9 § 1 State Secrets Law). A special Commission for Secrets Protection Co-ordination was created through Article 12 State Secrets Law. This Commission has, i.a., competence to issue certificates and to settle disputes concerning e.g., classification of information (Article 12 § 3 sub 2 and 7 State Secrets Law).

Procedural Rules

An applicant must submit a request for access to an official document in writing, including name and address. The institution concerned must reply within 14 days. If necessary, this term can be extended by another 14 days. The total period may not exceed one month (Article 10 Information Law). An institution that refuses a request must clearly justify its refusal. If a request is addressed to the wrong authority, it will be forwarded within three working days to the right authority (Article 12).

According to Article 11 § 2 Information Law, the applicant has the right to access the *original* document when possible. Otherwise, the institution should provide a copy or an extract. If full access to a document is not possible, the applicant will receive partial information or the part of the document not covered by an exception (Article 11).

Legal Remedies

According to Article 14 Information Law, the applicant has the right to appeal to the Administrative Disputes Commission.[123] The decision of this Commission is subject to appeal to the Administrative Court.

Other Characteristics

State and municipal institutions and agencies are – according to Article 6 § 2 PIP and Article 4 Information Law – obliged to inform the public of their activities. Institutions must prepare and publish information or otherwise disseminate information concerning their functions, structure and actual questions. Such information is publicly available and free of charge. Institutions have to maintain and make public a register of documents which they possess (Article 4 § 2 Information Law).

---

[123] The Commission's website can be found at http://www.vagk.lt/eng/index.php.

Malta

General Legislation on Access to Information[124]

Malta has no general legislation in the field of freedom of information or access to administrative documents. Freedom of information is addressed in two provisions: Article 41 of the Maltese Constitution of 1964 and Article 10 of the European Convention Act of 1987 (ECA).[125] Both provisions concern the freedom of expression, which includes the freedom to receive ideas and information without governmental interference. This freedom, however, cannot be construed as granting individuals a right to access to documents that are not voluntarily disclosed by the government. Considering that the ECA incorporates the European Convention on Human Rights and fundamental freedoms (ECHR) in the Maltese legal order, and that Article 10 of the ECA corresponds to Article 10 of the ECHR, case law of the European Court of Human Rights (ECtHR) must be taken into account. The ECtHR ruled in *Leander v. Sweden*[126] that Article 10 ECHR is intended to protect the free flow of information between individuals. Article 10 ECHR does not obligate a government to disclose information to an individual. The ECHR does not exclude that disclosure is obligatory when the applicant can show a personal interest in the disclosure of certain information. However, this is not covered by Article 10 ECHR, but in case of access to personal data by Article 8 ECHR, the right to privacy, or in case of information which is essential to assess to what risk someone is exposed by Article 2 ECHR, the right to life.[127]

Specific Legislation on Access to Information

Five regulations are worth mentioning: the Press act of 1974[128], the National Archives Act of 1990 (NAA)[129], the Ombudsman Act of 1995[130], the Environment Protection Act of 2001 and the Data Protection Act of 2002. The last two acts implement European legislation in this field and are not discussed here.[131]

---

[124] The majority of the information concerning freedom of information in Malta is taken from K. Aquilina, *Freedom of Information under Maltese Law*, 2003, published at http://www.humanrightsinitiative.org/programs/ai/rti/international/laws_papers/malta/foi_malta.pdf.

[125] See Aquilina (2003).

[126] See ECtHR 26 March 1987, *Leander v. Sweden*, appl. no. 9248/81, Series A, vol. 116.

[127] See ECtHR 7 July 1989, *Gaskin v. the United Kingdom*, appl. no. 10454/83, Series A, vol. 160 and ECtHR 18 June 2002, *Öneryildiz v. Turkey*, appl. no. 48939/99, n.y.p.

[128] An English translation of the Press Act of 23 August 1974 can be found at http://www.privacyinternational.org/countries/malta/press%20act%20chapt248.pdf.

[129] An English translation of the National Archives Act of 1st June 1990 can be found at http://www.education.gov.mt/ministry/doc/pdf/national_archives_act.pdf.

[130] An English translation of the Ombudsman Act of 25 July 1995 can be found at http://docs.justice.gov.mt/lom/legislation/english/leg/vol_11/chapt385.pdf.

[131] See in general the introduction on p. 3.

The Press Act states in Article 47 that:

> 1) The Government shall establish procedures to give representatives of the press the information which helps them fulfil their public tasks.
> 2) Subarticle (1) shall not apply in the following cases:
> (a) where such information could foil, impede, delay or jeopardise the appropriate process of pending legal proceedings or where Government or another public authority would be legally entitled to refuse to grant such information in a court or other tribunal established by law;
> (b) where the granting of such information would entail the disclosure of information received by Government in confidence;
> (c) where such information would violate an overriding public interest or a private interest warranting protection;
> (d) where the information concerns matters related to national security or public safety;
> (e) when the gathering of the information requested would place a disproportionate burden on the public administration.
> 3) It shall not be lawful for the Government to issue general instructions that prohibit the giving of information to any newspaper or licensed broadcasting service holding a particular view or to any specified newspaper or licensed broadcasting service.

The Ombudsman may, in accordance with Article 19 of the Ombudsman Act, from time to time require any person who in his opinion is able to give information relating to a matter that is being investigated by him to furnish him any such information, and to produce any documents or papers or things which relate to the investigation and which may be in the possession or under the control of that person. However, this competence is limited by Article 20 Ombudsman Act. Information will not be disclosed to the Ombudsman where the Prime Minister certifies that the giving of information (a) affects the security or defence of Malta, or international relations, (b) is likely to damage seriously the national economy, or (c) involves the disclosure of the deliberations or proceedings of the Cabinet or any committee of the Cabinet or (d) prejudices the investigation or detection of offences. In principle, the Ombudsman shall not disclose obtained information (Article 21 Ombudsman Act).

The national archives store administrative and departmental documents of the government of Malta, including all documents of the ministries, government commissions, authorities and boards. These documents are archived after a thirty-year period, as from the moment the document is no longer used for administrative purposes (Article 4 § 1 sub e NAA). The head of an institution has discretion as to whether to archive materials.[132] The Minister of education

[132] See Aquilina (2003), p. 5-6.

can limit access to certain archived documents where in his discretion they contain information that has been obtained by a public authority under an obligation of secrecy or confidentiality, or where the security of the State or the personal safety of any individual so require (Article 8 NAA).

Conclusion

In Malta, all documents held by government bodies are secret, unless provided otherwise in specific legislation or unless they have been stored in the National Archives and access is not limited by the Minister of education.[133]

[133] See also Aquilina (2003), p. 8. See for a non-legal point of view on freedom of information in Malta J. Borg, *Standard bearers, oasis seekers and wily contestants: Socio-cultural aspects of the right to information in Malta*, 2003, published at http://www.humanrightsinitiative.org/programs/ai/rti/international/laws_papers/malta/joeborg_malta.pdf.

The Netherlands

Legislation on Access to Information

- Article 110 of the Dutch Constitution[134]
- Act on the public access to government information of 31 October 1991[135]

Scope

According to Article 110 of the Dutch Constitution, government bodies shall – in the exercise of their duties – respect the right of public access to information in accordance with rules proscribed by the Act of Parliament on the public access to government information (Information Act). According to section 3, anyone may apply to an administrative authority, agency, or company carrying out work for an administrative authority, for information contained in documents concerning an administrative matter. According to section 1 sub a Information Act, 'document' means a written document or a material containing data that is deposited with an administrative authority. 'Administrative authority' is further specified in section 1a, namely:

a. The Ministers;
b. the administrative authorities of provinces, municipalities, water boards and regulatory industrial organisations;
c. administrative authorities whose activities are subject to the responsibility of the authorities referred to in subsection 1 (a and b);
d. such other administrative authorities as are not excluded by order in council.

The judiciary and the parliament are excluded. An 'administrative matter' is a matter of relevance to the policies of an administrative authority, including the preparation and implementation of such policies (section 1 sub b Information Act).

An administrative authority is under the explicit obligation – in the exercise of its functions – to disclose information in accordance with the Information Act (section 2 Information Act).

Point of Departure

Applications for information shall be granted, unless exceptions provided by law apply.

---

[134] An English translation of the Dutch Constitution can be found at http://www.oefre.unibe.ch/law/icl/nl00000_.html.

[135] An English translation of the Act can be found at http://www.aip-bg.org/documents/wob.htm.

Exceptions

The Information Act only contains mandatory exceptions, i.e., disclosure *shall* not take place. Some of these exceptions are subject to a harm test and some require a balancing of interests.

According to section 10 Information Act, disclosure shall not take place where:

a. this might endanger the unity of the Crown;
b. this might damage the security of the State;
c. the data concerned relates to companies and manufacturing processes and were furnished to the government in confidence by natural or legal persons.
d. the date is personal data, as meant in section 2 of chapter 2 of the Protection of personal data act, unless the disclosure clearly does not violate privacy.

Disclosure shall not occur where it does not outweigh one of the following:

a. relations between the Netherlands and other states or international organisations;
b. the economic and financial interests of the State, other bodies constituted under public law or the administrative authorities referred to in section 1a, subsection 1 (c and d) and subsection 2;
c. the investigation of criminal offences and the prosecution of offenders;
d. inspection, control and oversight by administrative authorities;
e. respect for personal privacy;
f. the importance to the addressee of being the first to note the information;
g. the prevention of disproportionate advantage or disadvantage to the natural or legal persons concerned or to third parties.

Special rules concerning internal documents are laid down in section 11 Information Act:

1. Where an application concerns information contained in documents drawn up for the purpose of internal consultation, no information shall be disclosed concerning personal opinions on policy contained therein.
2. Information on personal opinions on policy may be disclosed, in the interests of effective, democratic governance, in a form which cannot be traced back to any individual. If those who expressed the opinions in question or who supported them agree, information may be disclosed in a form which may be traced back to individuals.
3. Information concerning the personal opinions on policy contained in the recommendations of a civil service or mixed advisory committee may be disclosed if the administrative authority directly concerned informed the committee members of its intention to do so before they commenced their activities.

Procedural Rules

An applicant's oral or written request must specify the administrative matter concerned or the relevant document (section 3 § 2 Information Act). The applicant does not have to state reasons. If the request is in writing and addressed to the wrong authority, the request shall be forwarded to the right authority and the applicant will be so informed (section 4).

An administrative authority must answer a written request in writing (section 5 § 2). If the request was made orally, the applicant can ask for a notification in writing. The authority must answer as soon as possible, and in any event within two weeks after receipt of the request (section 6). Taking into account the applicant's preference, the authority can provide information by issuing a copy, permitting the applicant to take note of the contents of the document, supplying an extract from the document or by supplying the information contained in the document (section 7).

Legal Remedies

General rules on administrative procedure apply. The applicant must formally object to the decision of the administrative authority. The administrative authority reviews the application and makes a new decision. If the applicant is still unsatisfied with the outcome, he or she can appeal to the administrative court. The decision of this court can be overruled by the Administrative Jurisdiction Department of the Council of State.

Institutional Structure

Access to documents is not overseen by special supervisory authorities.

Other Characteristics

If disclosure of information on the policy of an administrative authority is in the interest of effective, democratic governance, the authority must on its own initiative disclose the information (section 8 § 1). The authority must ensure that the information is supplied in a comprehensible form and in such a way as to reach the interested party and as many interested members of the public as possible in time to allow them to make their views known to the authority (section 8 § 2).

Poland

Legislation on Access to Information

- Article 61 of the Polish Constitution of 2 April 1997[136]
- Act on Access to Public Information of 6 September 2001[137]
- Classified Information Protection Act of 22 January 1999[138]

Scope

Article 61 § 1-3 of the Polish Constitution reads:

> 1. A citizen shall have the right to obtain information on the activities of organs of public authority as well as persons discharging public functions. Such right shall also include receipt of information on the activities of self-governing economic or professional organs and other persons or organisational units relating to the field in which they perform the duties of public authorities and manage communal assets or property of the State Treasury.
> 2. The right to obtain information shall ensure access to documents and entry to sittings of collective organs of public authority formed by universal elections, with the opportunity to make sound and visual recordings.
> 3. Limitations upon the rights referred to in paras. 1 and 2 above, may be imposed by statute solely to protect freedoms and rights of other persons and economic subjects, public order, security or important economic interests of the State.

This article has led to the adoption of the Act on Access to Public Information (Information Act). Where the Constitution uses the word 'citizen', Article 2 of the Information Act grants *anyone,* including institutions, the right to access public information. The Information Act contains a mixture of active and passive distribution of information by public authorities.[139]

According to the Information Act, the right to information includes the right to obtain public information, examine official documents and access the

---

[136] An English translation of the Constitution can be found at http://www.sejm.gov.pl/english/konstytucja/kon1.htm.

[137] An English translation of this Act can be found at http://home.online.no/~wkeim/files/poland-foia.htm.

[138] An English translation of this Act can be found at http://faculty.maxwell.syr.edu/asroberts/foi/library/poland_secrecy.pdf.

[139] Disclosure of public information will take place by publishing it in the Public Information Bulletin (Biuletyn Informacji Publicznej). This Bulletin can be found at http://www.bip.gov.pl/. For an extensive analysis of the Polish Freedom of Information Act in relation to European legislation and some national legislation see the legal opinion prepared by J. Tallineau, *European Standards on access to Public Information,* 3 May 2003, to be found at http://www2.ukie.gov.pl/HLP/files.nsf/0/5C246E9FB841CE45C1256E8400369D5A/$file/039_Access_to_public_information_ENG.pdf.

sessions of collective public authority agencies elected by ballot (Article 3). The duty to disclose information applies to public authorities and other entities performing public tasks (Article 4). These rules also apply to trade unions and political parties. The notion of 'information' or 'documents' is not further specified.

Article 6 provides an extensive list of information that is accessible. For example, accessible information on the operating framework of public authorities includes:

a) procedures of public authorities and their organisational units,
b) procedures of state legal entities and territorial local government legal entities in the scope of performing public tasks and their activities in the scope of budget and extra budget economy,
c) methods of issuing public law acts,
d) methods of accepting and handling matters,
e) the status of accepted matters, order of their handling or deciding,
f) registers, records and archives kept and methods and principles of accessing data contained therein.[140]

Point of Departure

All information is accessible, unless exceptions provided by law apply.

Exceptions

According to Article 5 § 1 Information Act, the right to public information is subject to restrictions as provided by law. One of these is the Classified Information Protection Act (CIPA), which is discussed below. The right to public information – according to Article 5 § 2 Information Act – may be restricted by concerns regarding the privacy of natural persons or business secrets.

The CIPA defines the standards and requirements for safeguarding information expressed in whatever form and manner, including information that is being developed and which must be protected against unauthorised disclosure because it is a state secret or public service secret (together called 'classified information') (Article 1 CIPA). A 'state secret' is information whose disclosure may gravely threaten expose to no less than a substantial damage fundamental interests of the Republic of Poland, in particular the independence or inviolability of the territory, national defence and the security of the state and citizens (Article 2 § 1 CIPA). A 'public service secret' means classified information, other than a state secret, which has been obtained in connection with official duties or performance of agency contracts, whose unauthorised disclosure would damage interests of the state, public interests, or lawfully protected interests of citizens or organisations (Article 2 § 2 CIPA). Classified information may only be

[140] Article 6 § 3 Information Act.

disclosed to persons performing a specific duty or to those with special permission.

The classification of documents is done by the person authorised to sign a certain document (Article 21 CIPA). Annex I to the CIPA contains a list of categories of classified information. Annex II has a questionnaire for persons requesting permission.[141]

Procedural Rules

According to Article 10 Information Act, public information that is not already disclosed shall be accessible by application. Public information that is immediately accessible can be requested either orally or in writing without need for a written application. Access is granted without undue delay, at least within fourteen days from the receipt of the request (Article 13 § 1). If this time limit is exceeded, the authority must inform the applicant of the reasons for the delay and set another date, to be within two months (Article 13 § 2). In principle, access must be granted in the form that the applicant requested, unless technical means prevent the authority form doing so (Article 14). Refusal of access occurs by decision.

Legal Remedies

The provisions of the Polish Code of Administrative Procedure apply to the (negative) decision of the public authority (Article 16 Information Act). Applicants may request administrative review and eventually lodge an appeal to the administrative court.

Institutional Structure

With the entering into force of the CIPA, the Council of Ministers' Classified Information Security Committee was created in accordance with Article 5 CIPA. This Committee gives opinions and advises on matters concerning classified information.

[141] Both Annexes can be found at http://faculty.maxwell.syr.edu/asroberts/foi/library/poland_secrecy.pdf.

Portugal

Legislation on Access to Information

- Article 48 and 268 of the Portuguese Constitution[142]
- Act no. 65/93 on access to administrative documents of 26 August 1993[143]
- Act 6/94 on State Secrecy of 7 April 1994

Scope

Article 268 of the Portuguese Constitution states:

> 1. Citizens are entitled to be informed by the Public Service, when they so require, about the progress of proceedings in which they are directly interested and to know the final decisions that are taken with respect to them.
> 2. Citizens shall also enjoy the right to have access to administrative records and files, subject to the legal provisions with respect to internal and external security, investigation of crime and personal privacy.
> 3. Administrative action shall be notified to interested parties in the manner prescribed by law; it shall be based on stated and accessible substantial grounds when it affects legally protected rights or interests.
> 4. Interested parties are guaranteed effective protection of the courts for their legally protected rights or interests, including recognition of these rights or interests, challenging any administrative action, regardless of its form, that affects these, enforcing administrative acts that are legally due and adopting appropriate protective measures.
> [...]
> 6. For the purposes of paragraphs 1 and 2, the law shall fix the maximum period within which the Public Service must respond.

Paragraph 2 of this article has led to the adoption of Act no. 65/93 on access to administrative documents (Act 65/93). At first sight, the right of access to administrative documents seems to be restricted to Portuguese citizens. Not only does Article 268 of the Constitution speak of citizens, but also Article 1 Act 65/93 states that access to administrative documents *by the citizens* shall be ensured by the public administration according to the principles of publicity, transparency, equality, justice and impartiality. However, according to Article 7, *everyone* shall have the right to access information. The right to access applies to documents held or created by organs of either the State or the autonomous regions that perform administrative functions, by organs of either public institutes or public associations, organs of the local authorities, organs of associa-

[142] An English translation of the Constitution *before* the amendment of 2001 can be found at http://www.parlamento.pt/ingles/cons_leg/crp_ing/index.html.

[143] An English translation of the Act can be found via http://www.cada.pt.

tions or federations of local authorities, as well as other entities that exercise public authority according to the law (Article 3 § 1).

'Administrative documents' means any support of information, either graphic, aural, visual or computerised, or any record of another nature, augmented or held by the public administration, including files, reports, studies, opinions, minutes, official records, circulars, circular letters, internal orders, internal normative decisions, instructions and guidelines for the interpretation of the law or for setting the framework for an activity, as well as other pieces of information (Article 4 § 1 sub a). Personal notes, memos or other records of a similar nature, or documents that do not regard administrative activities, in particular documents concerning the meetings of the Council of Ministers and Secretaries of State, or which regard preparation for such meetings, is not considered administrative information (Article 4 § 2).

Access to documents concerning matters covered by secrecy of judicial procedures falls outside the scope of Act 65/93 and is regulated in special legislation (Article 6).

Point of Departure

Anyone may access administrative documents, unless exceptions provided by law are applicable.

Exceptions

According to Article 5 Act 65/93, documents containing information whose disclosure would create a risk for or be harmful to the State's internal or external security are classified according to special legislation. For a strict period of time, access to such documents may be denied or subject to authorisation. Act 6/94 on State Secrecy regulates this area. The denial of access to classified information is not automatic. A well-founded and concrete act of classification is necessary. A document may be considered secret for a maximum of four years. After the expiry of this period, secrecy can be invoked for another maximum period of four years.[144]

Act 65/93 draws a distinction between documents containing personal data, and documents that do not. Access to the first category is only granted to the person involved, or a third party which has either obtained written authorisation or can prove to have a direct, personal and legitimate interest (Article 8). Access to documents not containing personal information is in principle authorised.

An administrative authority may refuse access to documents if disclosure jeopardises commercial or industrial secrets or secrets relating to a company's internal affairs (Article 10).

[144] This information is taken from the general information on access to administrative documents in Portugal provided for by the Committee of Access to Administrative Documents. This information can be found at http://www.cada.pt/paginas/acessoing.html.

Procedural Rules

Requests for access to documents must be made in writing and must contain all references necessary for identifying the document, as well as the name, address and signature of the applicant (Article 13 Act 65/93). Documents may be accessed through on the spot consultation or reproduction through photocopy or any other technical means (Article 12).

Each ministerial department, regional department, local authority, institute and public association has an entity that is responsible for the implementation of Act 65/93 (Article 14). This entity must answer a request within a period of ten days (Article 15 § 1). If the request concerns documents that contain third party personal information and this party gave no prior authorisation, the responsible entity must request an opinion from the Committee of Access to Administrative Documents (CADA, see below).

Legal Remedies

Within 20 days, an applicant may submit a complaint to the CADA regarding a public authority's rejection of a request (Article 16 § 1 Act 65/93). The CADA will draw up a report within 30 days, which will be forwarded to all interested persons (Article 16 § 2). After receiving this report, the public authority gives a new answer. It must include reasons on which the decision is based (Article 16 § 3).

The latter decision is subject to appeal to the administrative courts (Article 17 Act). Also, failure to reply to an application is subject to appeal.

Institutional Structure

In accordance with Article 18, a Committee of Access to Administrative Documents was created.[145] The Committee is entrusted with overseeing implementation of Act 65/93. The CADA can examine complaints, provide opinions on access, review practices and decide on the system of classifying documents. However, CADA decisions are not legally binding on public authorities (Article 20). The CADA produces an annual report. All staff members working for public authorities are obliged to co-operate with the CADA (Article 21).

Other Characteristics

Both the Constitution and Act 65/93 contain rules on the active disclosure of information.

In Article 48 of the Constitution, this is formulated as every citizen's right to objective information about state and public body activities and a right to be informed by the government and other authorities about the management

[145] CADA's website can be found at http://www.cada.pt/.

of public affairs. According to Article 11 Act 65/93, the administration shall publish through adequate means:

a) any documents, including internal normative decisions, circulars and guidelines, that contain structures for the administrative activity;
b) reference to any documents containing an interpretation of enacted laws or a description of an administrative procedure, including in that reference *inter alia* the title and date of the documents, the subject and the originator thereof, as well as the place where the documents may be consulted.

Slovak Republic

Legislation on Access to Information

- Article 26 of the Slovak Constitution of 1 September 1992[146]
- Act no. 211/00 on Free Access to Information of 17 May 2000, entered into force on 1 January 2001[147]
- Act no. 215/04 on Protection of Classified Information of 11 March 2004[148]

Scope

Article 26 § 1 of the Slovak Constitution guarantees freedom of speech and the right to information. The scope of the latter must be seen in light of § 4 and 5:

> 4) The freedom of speech and the right to seek out and spread information can be restricted by law if such a measure is unavoidable in a democratic society to protect the rights and liberties of others, state security, public order, or public health and morality.
> 5) State bodies and territorial self-administration bodies are under an obligation to provide information on their activities in an appropriate manner and in the state language. The conditions and manner of execution will be specified by law.

With regard to environmental information, Article 45 of the Constitution grants everyone the right to timely and complete information about the state of the environment and the causes and consequences of its condition.

Detailed rules on access to information can be found in Act no. 211/00 on Free Access to Information (Act 211/00). According to Article 3 Act 211/00, *everybody* – including legal persons – shall have the right to access information that obligees have available. 'Obligees' are entities obliged to provide access to information under Act 211/00. These entities consist of state agencies, municipalities, as well as legal entities and natural persons that have been given the power by law to make decisions on the rights and responsibilities of natural persons or legal entities in the area of public administration (Article 2 § 1). This obligation applies only to the decision-making power of these entities.

Act 211/00 draws a distinction between 'disclosed information' – information that is always accessible – and 'associated information'. The latter means information that is closely related to requested information, including information on the mere existence of the information, its origin, number, but also

---

[146] An English translation of the Slovak Constitution can be found at http://www.oefre.unibe.ch/law/icl/looooo_.html.

[147] An English translation of this Act can be found at http://www.info211.sk/zakon_en.php.

[148] An English translation of this Act can be found at http://www.nbusr.sk/index_en.php.

possible reasons for denial of access to the requested information and the period of denial.

Article 5 contains an extensive list of information whose disclosure is mandatory. Disclosure must take place in a way that enables 'mass access', meaning accessibility by means of telecommunications, especially through the Internet (Article 4 § 2 and 6 § 1).

Point of Departure

Everyone has the right to access information that public authorities have made available, unless exceptions provided by law apply.

Exceptions

Exceptions to the right of access to information can be found in Articles 8 through 11 Act 211/00. If the requested information is classified in accordance with Act no 215/04 on Protection of Classified Information (Act 215/04), access on the basis of Act 211/00 shall be denied (Article 8 Act 211/00). According to Article 2 of Act 215/04, classified material is specified as such by the originator of the material. Classified information is information whose disclosure would be detrimental to the interests of the Slovak Republic or to interests that the Slovak Republic has been committed to protect. Only specifically authorised persons can access classified information.

Information containing personal data may be disclosed only when so ordered by a special act[149] or by the prior consent of the person concerned (Article 9 Act 211/00). Information classified as a state secret shall not be disclosed (Article 10). Furthermore, the obligee shall limit disclosure or not provide information if:

a) information was obtained from a person not required by law to provide information, who upon notification of the Obligee instructed the Obligee in writing not to disclose information. If the person authorized to give consent for disclosure of information fails to reply within 7 days upon notification, it shall be deemed that the person consented to disclosure of information. The person must be informed of the consequences in the notification,
b) information is to be disclosed under a special act; and if it is to be disclosed under such law within a period set in advance; and not later than such period,
c) it may violate intellectual property rights under a special law, except if the author consented to the disclosure of information upon notification of the Obligee,
d) it concerns the decision-making power of the courts and law enforcement bodies,

[149] See Act no. 428/2002 on Personal Data Protection of 3 July 2002, an English translation can be found at http://www.dataprotection.gov.sk/buxus/docs/act_no_428.pdf.

e) it concerns the place of habitat of endangered species of plants and animals, minerals and fossils and there is a threat of inappropriate destruction, damage or disturbance.[150]

The entitlement to refuse access to information shall last only as long as the reasons for non-disclosure exist (Article 12).

Procedural Rules

An application may be filed in writing or orally. A request must contain the details of the authority it is addressed to, the name of the applicant, what information is requested and in what way disclosure is to be made (Article 14 § 1 Act 211/00). If an applicant fails to fulfil these requirements, the authority shall inform the applicant within seven days. The authority must instruct an applicant on how to complete a request (Article 14 § 3). Applicants are not obliged to provide legal or other reasons or interests when applying for information (Article 3 § 3).

In case the application is sent to the wrong authority, this authority shall pass on the request to the right authority (Article 15). The authority has to answer the request with undue delay, but not later than ten days (Article 17 § 1). For serious reasons this period can be extended by ten days (Article 17 § 2).

Legal Remedies

If access is granted, no appeal is possible against this decision (Article 18 § 1 Act 211/00). If access is refused, the authority's decision is subject to an administrative appeal by the authority's superior (Article 19 § 1 and 2). The superior body's decision is subject to appeal to the administrative court (Article 19 § 4). A public official violating the provisions of Act 211/00 can be fined up to SKK 50.000 (Article 23).

Other Characteristics

In accordance with Article 20 Act 211/00, the obligees keep a registry of requests.

Other Activities in the Field of Transparency

Research on how Act 211/00 works in practise is carried out by NGOs, for example, *Aliancia Fair-Play*.[151]

---

[150] Article 11 § 1 Act 211/00.

[151] See the website of Aliancia Fair-Play in Slovakian at http://www.fair-play.sk/index.php.

Slovenia

Legislation on Access to Information

- Article 38 and 39 of the Slovenian Constitution of 23 December 1991[152]
- Act on the access to information of public character of 25 February 2003[153]
- Classified Information Act, entered into force on 23 November 2001[154]

Scope

Article 39 § 2 of the Slovenian Constitution reads:

> (2) Except in such cases as are provided by law, everyone has the right to obtain information of a public nature in which he has a well founded legal interest under law.

A right to access to personal data is provided for in Article 38 § 3 of the Constitution:

> Everyone has the right of access to the collected personal data that relates to him and the right to judicial protection in the event of any abuse of such data.

The Act on the access to information of a public character (Information Act) is based on Article 39 of the constitution. The aim of the Information Act is to ensure the publication and openness of the work of public bodies, as well as to facilitate the exercise of the rights of individuals and legal entities to acquire information of a public character. With a view to achieve the aim of this Act, public bodies try to inform the public on their work to the greatest extent possible (Article 2). According to Article 5 of the Act, legal entities and natural persons have free access to information of a public character that is held by public bodies.

Public bodies are state bodies, local government bodies, public agencies, public funds and other entities of public law, holders of public powers and public service contractors (Article 1). Annually, the Slovenian government publishes a list of what entities are considered public bodies. 'Information of public character' means information originating from the work of public bodies and occurring in the form of a document, case, dossier, register, record or documentary material that is created in co-operation with other bodies, or acquired from other persons (Article 4).

---

[152] An English translation of the Constitution can be found at http://www.oefre.unibe.ch/law/icl/si00000_.html.

[153] An English translation of the Act can be found at http://unpan1.un.org/intradoc/groups/public/documents/UNTC/UNPAN015727.pdf.

[154] An English translation of the Act can be found at http://nato.gov.si/eng/documents/classified-info-act/.

Point of Departure

Information of public character is accessible, unless otherwise provided by law.

Exceptions

Exceptions on accessibility are listed in Article 6 Information act. A public body shall refuse access if the application relates to:

1. Information which, pursuant to the Act governing classified data, is defined as classified for the purposes of public security, national security, confidentiality of international relations or confidentiality of intelligence and security activities of state bodies;
2. Information which is defined as a business secret in accordance with the Act governing companies;
3. Personal data the disclosure of which would constitute an infringement of the protection of personal data in accordance with the Act governing the protection of personal data;
4. Information the disclosure of which would constitute an infringement of the confidentiality of individual information on reporting units, in accordance with the Act governing Government statistics activities;
5. Information from the public archives material which is, in accordance with the Act governing archives material and archives, defined as confidential;
6. Information the disclosure of which would constitute an infringement of the tax procedure confidentiality in accordance with the Act governing tax procedure;
7. Information acquired or drawn up for the purposes of criminal prosecution or in relation to criminal prosecution, or misdemeanours procedure, and the disclosure of which would prejudice the implementation of such procedure;
8. Information acquired or drawn up for the purposes of administrative procedure, and the disclosure of which would prejudice the implementation of such procedure;
9. Information acquired or drawn up for the purposes of civil, non-litigious civil procedure or other court proceedings, and the disclosure of which would prejudice the implementation of such procedures;
10. Information from the document that is in the process of drawing up and is still subject of consultation in a body, and the disclosure of which would lead to misunderstanding of its contents;
11. Information on natural value which, in accordance with the Act governing the conservation of nature, is not accessible to public for the purpose of protection of natural value;
12. Information from the document drawn up in connection with internal operations or activities of bodies, and the disclosure of which would lead to disturbances in operations or activities of an body.

Interestingly, Article 26 Information Act states that public bodies *may* refuse a request if it finds the requested information or document to be an exception under Article 6 Information Act. If only part of the information falls under an exception, this part shall be removed and the remaining part of the information shall be released (Article 7).

Article 6 § 1 of the Act refers to the Classified Information Act (CIA). This Act provides rules on classified information for reasons of public security, defence, foreign affairs, intelligence and security (Article 1 CIA). An authorised person may classify information under the conditions and manner specified by the CIA (Article 10 CIA). Access to classified information is possible only with permission granted after a security clearance (chapter III CIA).

Procedural Rules

Applicants may request access to information in writing or orally (Article 12 Information Act). The request must indicate the public body where it is being filed, the applicant's name (including the name of a company or legal entity) and address (Article 17 § 1). In the request, the applicant must specify the desired information and the manner of transmittal (consultation on the spot, a transcript, a copy, an electronic record) (Article 17 § 2). The applicant is not required to state legal grounds for the request or expressly characterise it as a request for information of public character. From the nature of the request, it follows that such information is of a public character under the Information Act. The public body must consider the request pursuant to the Information Act (Article 17 § 3). If these procedural conditions are not met, the public body shall dismiss the request by order (Article 19).

Each public body shall appoint one or more officials responsible for the transmission of information of a public character (Article 9). These officials immediately decide upon a request, at the latest within twenty working days (Article 23). Exceptional circumstances mentioned in Article 24 can justify the extending of this period to a maximum of thirty working days. If the public body wholly or partly refuses access to the information, it shall issue a written decision (Article 22). This decision must contain an explanation of the grounds for refusal as well as advice on legal remedies.

Legal Remedies

An applicant has the right to appeal a decision refusing a request to the Commissioner on Access to Information of Public Character (Article 27 Information Act). An appeal to a court can be lodged against the Commissioner's decision (Article 31). Public bodies non-compliance with the Information Act can lead to fines of at least SIT 250 000 (Article 39).

Institutional Structure

Since 2003, the Commissioner on Access to Information of Public Character has operated pursuant to Articles 27 through 30 Information Act.[155] Under these provisions, the Commissioner only appears competent to decide upon appeals (Article 28 § 1).

In 2001, the Ministry of Information Society was established. Its main task was to promote the development and use of information and communications technology throughout Slovenia. The Ministry of Information Society dealt with matters pertaining to informatics and information systems, development of information technology, promotion of an information society and electronic commerce, post and telecommunications traffic, telecommunication links and systems, and innovation. In its broad field of information activities, the Ministry also dealt with the implementation and promotion of the Information Act. In November 2004 the Ministry ceased to exist. The tasks of the Ministry were distributed over different ministries.[156]

Other Characteristics

The Information Act contains provisions on the active disclosure of information of public character. According to Article 8, every public body is obliged to maintain and make public a register of public information. Article 10 obliges public bodies to transmit to the World Wide Web information of public character. This includes consolidated texts of regulations that relate to the body's activities, with regard to the state register of regulations on the Web, programmes, strategies, views, opinions, studies, and other similar documents relating to the body's activities, proposals for regulations, programmes, strategies, and other similar documents, all publications and tendering documentation in accordance with regulations governing public procurements, information on administrative services and other information of public character. The scope of this obligation seems to be unlimited, since 'other information of public character' also falls within the ambit of the obligation (Article 10 § 6).

According to Article 32, the Ministry shall promote and develop access to information of a public character i.a. by informing the public of the means and conditions of access to information and by providing counselling to other bodies on the proper application of the Information Act. Article 37 Information Act obliges public bodies to create an annual report on the implementation of the Information Act. Each year, the government publishes a joint report (Article 37 § 3).[157]

---

155 The Commissioner's website can be found at http://www.dostopdoinformacij.si/index.php?id=149.

156 The Ministry of Information Society website can still be found at http://www.uvi.si/eng/slovenia/publications/facts/information/.

157 To be found in Slovenian at http://193.2.236.12/mid/mid.nsf/V/KB8C7C4223B9B6B7CC1256E69003C139D/$file/Skupno_letno_porocilo_ZDIJZ_Vlada01042004.pdf.

Spain

Legislation on Access to Information

- Article 105 (b) of the Spanish Constitution[158]
- Article 37 Act no. 30 on rules for public administration and administrative procedures of 26 November 1992[159]

Scope

Article 105 (b) of the Spanish Constitution states that the law shall regulate citizens' access to administrative files and records, except where they may concern the security and defence of the State, the investigation of crimes and the individual privacy.

This article has led to Act no. 30 on rules for public administration and administrative procedures (Act 30/92). This act provides that *citizens* have a right to access to records and documents that are part of a file and which are held in the administrative archives in whatever form, be it graphic, audio or visual (Article 37 § 1 Act 30/92). The files must pertain to matters that have been concluded at the time of the request; accordingly, preparatory documents are not accessible (Article 37 § 1 Act 30/92).

Access to documents containing information on the private lives of individuals is restricted to the persons concerned (Article 37 § 2 Act 30/92). Article 37 § 3 grants access to documents with a nominative character that do not contain private information. These documents must be part of implementing legislation and must contain information that may be invoked through the exercise of civil rights. Such documents may be consulted by concerned persons or by third parties who prove a legitimate and direct interest, unless the material is of a disciplinary or penalising nature.

Point of Departure

All documents are accessible to citizens, unless provided otherwise by law.

Exceptions

The right of access may be refused for reasons of public interest, for the protection of third party interests, or when provided for by law. The authority concerned shall give reasons for refusal (Article 4 Act 30/92).

The right of access does not apply in the cases listed in § 5:

---

158 An English translation of the Constitution can be found at http://www.spainemb.org/information/constitucionin.htm.

159 The Spanish text of this Act can be found at http://noticias.juridicas.com/base_datos/Admin/l30-1992.html.

- to documents containing information on actions undertaken by the Government or the autonomous communities when exercising constitutional responsibilities which are not subject to administrative law;
- to documents containing information on national defence or State security;
- in connection with a criminal investigation, when disclosure of those documents might *jeopardise* the protection of the rights and freedoms of third parties, or the needs of the investigation being carried out;
- files relating to matters protected by business or industrial secrecy;
- files relating to administrative actions in connection with monetary policy.

Article 37 § 6 refers to situations that are governed by specific provisions, including i.a., access to archives containing classified material, access to documents and files that contain personal medical data, access to documents in the archives of the public administration when those who are trying to access are members of the parliament or are senators, and the consultation of documents housed in the Historical Archives.

Procedural Rules

The right to access documents must be exercised with due regard to the efficacy of public administration (Article 37 § 7 Act 30/92). Individuals must specify which document they want to access, or at least the topic on which they want information.

The right to documents entails the right to receive copies or certifications of the documents whose examination has been authorised by the administration (Article 37 § 8).

Legal Remedies

Refusals can be appealed administratively. The Spanish Ombudsman can also review cases.

Sweden

Legislation on Access to Information

- The Freedom of the Press Act (FPA) of 1766, amended in 1949 and 1976.[160] This act forms – as chapter 2 – part of the Swedish constitution. Specific rules concerning access to official documents are laid down in chapter 2 'On the Public Nature of Official Documents' of the FPA.
- The Secrecy Act of 1980[161]

Scope

Article 1 of chapter 2 of the FPA reads:

> Every Swedish citizen shall be entitled to have free access to official documents, in order to encourage the free exchange of opinion and the availability of comprehensive information.

Although this article suggests otherwise, access to information is not restricted to 'Swedish citizens'. Article 4 of chapter 14 of the FPA states that foreign nationals are equated with Swedish citizens, except as otherwise laid down in the FPA.

An 'official document', according to Article 3 of chapter 2 of the FPA, is any written or pictorial matter or recording which may be read, listened to, or otherwise accessed through technical aids. A documents is 'official' if it is held by a public authority, and if it is received or drawn up by such an authority. The Riksdag and local government assemblies vested with decision-making powers are public authorities (Article 5). The government or local government assemblies have the ability to state by law that a document should remain official even where it is transferred to a private body which assumes public authority (Article 17). These private bodies are equated with public authorities when applying Articles 12 through 16, which lay down procedural rules. Internal documents (for example memoranda, preliminary outlines or drafts of decisions) that have not been dispatched by a public authority are not considered to be 'official documents', unless they have been filed and registered (Article 9).

Point of Departure

The Freedom of the Press Act suggests that openness is the rule and secrecy is the exception.[162]

---

[160] An English translation of this Act can be found at http://www.riksdagen.se/english/work/fundamental/press.asp.

[161] The Swedish text of this Act can be found at http://www.notisum.se/rnp/SLS/LAG/19800100.HTM.

[162] See Prakke & Kortmann (2004), p. 855/6 and I. Österdahl, *Openness v. Secrecy: Public Access to Documents in Sweden and the European Union*, in *E.L.Rev.* 1998, p. 336.

Exceptions

The exceptions are laid down in Article 2, chapter 2 FPA:

> The right of access to official documents may be restricted only if restriction is necessary having regard to:
> 1. the security of the Realm or its relations with another state or an international organisation;
> 2. the central fiscal, monetary or currency policy of the Realm;
> 3. the inspection, control or other supervisory activities of a public authority;
> 4. the interest of preventing or prosecuting crime;
> 5. the economic interest of the public institutions;
> 6. the protection of the personal or economic circumstances of private subjects;
> 7. the preservation of animal or plant species.

This limited list of – initially discretionary – restrictions is formulated in a general way. Before restrictions can be invoked, they must 'be scrupulously specified in a provision of a special act of law, or, if this is deemed more appropriate in a particular case, in another act of law to which the special act refers' (Article 2 § 2). The Riksdag or the government may be empowered to permit the release of a particular document, as regards the circumstances of a case (Article 2 § 3). The most important act in this respect is the Secrecy Act of 1980.[163] This Act distinguishes between absolute and relative secrecy. Absolute secrecy means that access to documents is denied from the moment the relevant interest applies.[164] However, the majority of the secrecy provisions are subject to a 'requirement of damage'. This harm test implies that the authority concerned must ask itself, *every time* someone asks for access to an official document, whether disclosure would truly harm the interest that is being protected by confidentiality. Time limits on secrecy can vary from two to seventy years, depending on the protected interest.[165]

Procedural Rules

Article 12, chapter 2 FPA reads:

> An official document to which the public has access shall be made available on request forthwith, or as soon as possible, at the place where it is held, and free

[163] Information about the Secrecy Acts is extracted from 'Public Access to Information and Secrecy with Swedish Authorities', which is published by the Ministry of Justice of Sweden, 2000, to be found at: http://www.sweden.se/upload/Sweden_se/english/publications/RK/PDF/RK_Public_access.pdf.

[164] Absolute secrecy applies, for example, to documents held by the Swedish tax authorities. See Österdahl (1998), p. 343.

[165] Ministry of Justice (2000), p. 20.

of charge, to any person wishing to examine it, in such a form that it can be read, listened to, or otherwise comprehended.

If part of a document contains classified material, the rest of the document is made available to the applicant in the form of a transcript or copy (Article 12). If disclosure presents serious difficulties for the public authorities, the obligation to disclose ceases to exist (Article 12). Applicants are entitled to obtain a copy or a transcript of the document, in return for a fixed fee (Article 13). This request must be dealt with promptly (Article 13). Public authorities are not obliged to disclose materials recorded for automatic data processing in any other form than a printout (Article 13). Authorities are not permitted to inquire into a person's identity or into the purpose of the request, except insofar as such inquiry is necessary to enable the authority to judge whether there is any obstacle to the release of the document (Article 14).

Legal Remedies

An applicant is generally entitled to appeal a *negative* decision on a request to access official documents. Appeals are usually presented to an administrative court of appeal. An appeal against a decision of the latter can be lodged with the Supreme Administrative Court.[166] Decisions by the Riksdag and the government cannot be appealed (Article 15). An appeal against a decision by a minister is lodged with the government (Article 15 FPA). Complaints can also be made to the Parliamentary Ombudsman. Decisions of the Ombudsman are, however, not binding.[167]

Institutional Structure

There are no special supervisory authorities in the field of access to documents.

Other Characteristics

Public authorities are obliged to register documents that they receive or create (chapter 15 of the Secrecy Act). Some exceptions to this obligation exist. Documents that are of obviously little importance to the authorities' activities are exempted. Documents that are not secret and are kept in such a matter that it can easily be ascertained whether they have been received or drawn up by the authority are also exempted. Exceptions also apply to documents that the authority has large quantities of, documents that the government has exempted from the registration requirement according to special provisions, and Electronic Data Processing (EDP) recordings which the authority has by reason of another authority having already registered them in a common EDP register.[168]

[166] Ministry of Justice (2000), p. 27.

[167] The Ombudsman's homepage can be found at http://www.jo.se/default.asp?SetLanguage=en.

[168] Ministry of Justice (2000), p. 26/7.

United Kingdom

Legislation on Access to Information

- Freedom of Information Act of 30 November 2000[169]
- Freedom of Information (Scotland) Act of 28 May 2002[170]

Scope

The Freedom of Information Act 2000 (FOIA) applies to the whole of the United Kingdom (UK) except for the public authorities of Scotland. Scotland has its own Freedom of Information Act. Below, the FOIA of the UK is described. With regard to the Scottish Freedom of Information Act, this inventory will only point to striking differences with the FOIA of the UK.

According to section 1 FOIA any person making a request for information to a public authority is entitled

> (a) to be informed in writing by the public authority whether it holds information of the description specified in the request, and
> (b) if that is the case, to have that information communicated to him.

'Public authority' means bodies, persons, or holders of an office listed in Schedule 1 or designated by order of Secretary of State (section 3 § 1 FOIA). The twenty-page list in Schedule 1 describes public authorities. The Secretary of State, through an amending order, may extend the list (section 5). Publicly owned companies are also considered public authorities (section 3 § 1 and 6). Information is held by a public authority if it is held by the authority otherwise than on behalf of another person, or if it is held by another person on behalf of the authority (section 3 § 2).

Section 87 states the date on which the FOIA will enter into force. Some sections enter into force on the day that the FOIA is passed, some at the end of a two-month period and others only after five years or on a such day before the end of that period as the Secretary of State may by order appoint. Section 1 and the sections containing the exceptions belong to the latter. These sections apply since 1 January 2005, the date on which the whole FOIA entered into force. Until that time, the voluntary Code of Practice on Access to Government Information of 1994 applied.[171]

---

169 To be found at http://www.hmso.gov.uk/acts/acts2000/20000036.htm.

170 To be found at http://www.scotland-legislation.hmso.gov.uk/legislation/scotland/acts2002/20020013.htm.

171 To be found at http://www.cfoi.org.uk/coptext.html.

Point of Departure

All information held by public authorities is accessible, unless exceptions provided by law apply.

Exceptions

An extensive list of exceptions is provided for in Part II (sections 21 to 44) of the FOIA. According to section 2, the grant of access to information does not apply if a) information falls within the ambit of mandatory exemptions, or b) the public interest in maintaining the exemption outweighs the public interest in disclosing the information.

The sections containing mandatory exceptions are exclusively listed in section 2 § 3:

- Section 21, information accessible to applicant by other means;
- Section 23, information supplied by, or relating to, bodies dealing with security measures;
- Section 32, court records;
- Section 34, parliamentary privilege;
- Section 36, prejudice to effective conduct of public affairs (this section is absolute so far as relating to information held by the House of Commons or the House of Lords);
- Section 40 § 1 and 2, personal information, (the absolute character of § 2 is subject to certain conditions);
- Section 41, information provided in confidence;
- Section 44, prohibitions on disclosure by or under any enactment or community law.

Apparently, all the other exceptions are subject to the balancing of interests. The remaining exceptions are:[172]

- Section 22, information intended for future publication;
- Section 24, national security;
- Section 26, defence (h);
- Section 27, international relations (h);
- Section 28, relations within the UK (h);
- Section 29, the economy (h);
- Section 30, investigations and proceedings conducted by public authorities;
- Section 31, law enforcement (h);
- Section 33, audit functions (h);
- Section 35, formulation of government policy;

[172] Exceptions requiring a harm test are indicated by '(h)'.

- Section 36, prejudice to effective conduct of public affairs (except for information held by the House of Commons or the House of Lords, see above) (h);
- Section 37, communications with Her Majesty, etc. and honours;
- Section 38, health and safety (h);
- Section 39, environmental information;
- Section 40, personal information (except for § 1, and § 2 under certain conditions, see above);
- Section 42, legal professional privilege;
- Section 43, commercial interests (h);

Public authorities do not have to comply with requests for information that are vexatious or where a request for information is made by the same person with regard to the same information, after the previous request was complied with (section 14).

Procedural Rules

A request for information must be made in writing, must contain the name of the applicant and an address for correspondence and must describe the information requested (section 8 FOIA). The public authority concerned can – in accordance with a regulation made by the Secretary of State – charge a fee (section 9). A 'fees notice' must be given to the applicant. The public authority is not obliged to handle a request as long as the applicant has not paid the fee.

The public authority concerned must comply with a request promptly and in any event not later than twenty working days after the receipt of the application (section 10). The public authority shall so far as reasonably practicable, give effect to the preference expressed by the applicant for the way in which the requested information is communicated (section 11). Public authorities have the duty to provide advice and assistance (section 16). In case of refusal, the authority shall give the applicant a notice which specifies the exemption in question and states why the exemption applies.

Legal Remedies

Any person may apply to the Information Commissioner for a decision whether a request has been dealt with by a public authority in conformity with the FOIA (section 50 § 1). The Commissioner can decide that the public authority has failed to fulfil its obligations under the FOIA and can specify which steps the authority must take for complying with the requirements (section 50 § 4). This decision can have the character of an 'enforcement notice', which is legally binding (section 52). However, according to Article 53 § 2, the enforcement notice shall cease to have effect if the accountable person in relation to the authority gives the Commissioner a certificate signed by him stating that he or she has on reasonable grounds formed the opinion that there was no failure to comply with the duty to make the information concerned available. In case of non-compliance with the enforcement notice, the Commissioner can bring the case before a court (section 54). When the Commissioner takes a decision, the applicant or the public authority may appeal to the Information Tribunal (section 57). Decisions of the Information Tribunal are subject to appeal on points of law to the High Court of Justice of England, the Court of Session of Scotland, or the High Court of Justice in Northern Ireland (section 59).

Institutional Structure

By virtue of section 18 FOIA, the former Data Protection Commissioner is renamed Information Commissioner and the former Data Protection Tribunal is renamed the Information Tribunal.[173] The Information Commissioner oversees, promotes and enforces the FOIA. On its own initiative, the Commissioner can give recommendations to public authorities (section 48).[174] Competence with regard to individual complaint is described above. Annually, the Commissioner submits a general report on the exercise of its function to each House of Parliament (section 49).

Other Characteristics

According to section 19 FOIA, every public authority is under the duty to adopt and maintain a scheme that relates to the authority's publication of information. Such a scheme must be approved by the Commissioner. A publication scheme must specify classes of information which the authority publishes or intends to publish, specify the manner in which information of each class is, or is intended to be, published, and specify whether the material is, or is intended to be, available to the public free of charge (section 19 § 2). The powers of the Commissioner with regard to publication schemes are laid down in section 20.

Part VI of the FOIA contains rules concerning historical records. Historical records are records that are more than thirty years old. After the lapse of the thirty-year period, some of the exceptions may no longer be applicable (section 63 to 65).

Other Activities in the Field of Transparency

One of the NGO's active in the field of freedom of information is the *Campaign for Freedom of Information* (CFI). This NGO campaigns against unnecessary official secrecy. The CFI monitors existing access rights by publishing reports and provides practical guides to help people use their rights.[175]

---

173 The Information Tribunal's website can be found at http://www.dca.gov.uk/foi/inftrib.htm.

174 The Commissioner's website can be found at http://www.informationcommissioner.gov.uk/.

175 The CFI's very informative website can be found at http://www.cfoi.org.uk/.

Freedom of Information Act of Scotland

The Scottish FOIA is based on the UK FOIA and is considered to provide more transparency than the UK act.[176] Some differences exist in the exceptions category. For example, the Scottish FOIA requires a (substantial) harm test in the case of information concerning national security and defence (section 31 FOIA), where the UK FOIA does not. Another difference between the two acts is the possibility for public authorities to give a certificate to the Commissioner, through which a Commissioner's decision ceases to have effect. In the Scottish FOIA, only the First Minister of the Scottish Executive is granted this power.

Like the UK Act, the Scottish FOIA will enter into force on 1 January 2005. The Scottish system has its own Scottish Information Commissioner.[177]

---

176 See D. Banisar (2004), p. 92.

177 The Scottish Information Commissioner's very informative website can be found at http://www.itspublicknowledge.info/.